Peace and Justice Shall Embrace

BOOKS BY A. COMPANION

- *Peace and Justice Shall Embrace: Toward Restorative Justice*

  Unparalleled practical, biblical and human critique of the U.S. criminal justice systems, with cogent proposals and models for restorative justice reforms. A cross-reference is provided to the U.S. Catholic bishops' statement on criminal justice: *Responsibility, Rehabilitation and Restoration.* ISBN: 0-595-17654-2

- *Wounded Wounders: Stories of Men in Prison*

  Powerful, poignant stories of men in prison told in their own words. These are stories of wounders—themselves wounded—stories of sin, hopelessness, grace and redemption. ISBN: 0-595-17674-7

These books may be ordered from iUniverse.com, Barnes & Noble (*www.bn.com*), Amazon.com or your bookstore.

Proceeds from the sale of these books go to Restoration House (a charitable non-profit corporation) to be established in Sacramento.

Restoration House Mission Statement

Restoration House is a spiritually based ministry of Christian compassion, love and healing. We provide a transitional community for men paroled from prison.

We are committed:
- to the restorative processes of reclaiming personal dignity;
- to facing and dealing with addictive and self-destructive patterns;
- to learning practical and social living skills;
- to the transition to employment and self-sufficiency as fully integrated, contributing members of society.

Peace and Justice Shall Embrace

Toward Restorative Justice…a Prisoner's Perspective

A. Companion

165101

Writers Club Press

San Jose New York Lincoln Shanghai

Peace and Justice Shall Embrace
Toward Restorative Justice...a Prisoner's Perspective

Writers Club Press
an imprint of iUniverse.com, Inc.

For information address:
iUniverse.com, Inc.
5220 S 16th, Ste. 200
Lincoln, NE 68512
www.iuniverse.com

ISBN: 0-595-17654-2

Printed in the United States of America

CONTENTS

PREFACE—THE AUTHOR

Overnight, with my unexpected arrest, my distant relationship to the systems of justice was traumatically inverted. I am a former Roman Catholic priest and I am writing from prison, not as a chaplain, but as a prisoner.

I was actively involved in social justice advocacy for over 30 years, but direct contact with criminal justice systems had been limited to a dozen pastoral visits to the county jail and juvenile hall, and about the same number of appearances in court to speak on behalf of a probation sentence. While preaching against capital punishment, it was totally beyond my purview to imagine having murderers, kidnappers and other felons as cell mates and friends. And it wasn't until I was driven into San Quentin State Prison in chains, that I was struck by the irony that not long before I had kept futile vigil there protesting a pending execution in its gas chamber.

This book is a continuation of my social justice ministry, but now informed by my firsthand experiences as a defendant and convict, and reflected upon from the perspective of the Gospel of Jesus Christ. Because I am a Catholic Christian, much of what I share will come from that world vision. It is my hope that readers who come to these issues from other world views will be enriched by what they read here, and will offer their own valued traditions and insights to enhance mine.

Again, because my personal experience has been within the justice and corrections systems of California, most references and proposals relate to conditions here. However, with minor differences, what is presented is mostly valid everywhere in the United States. Whereas the data given herein is constantly changing, the issues and principles reflected by them remain valid.

While I share personal life experiences herein, this is not my story, nor do I wish it to distract from the focus and purpose of this book. I will tell my story at a later time.

*   *   *

Beginning with arresting deputies at my door, to my present daily encounters with the brutal, dehumanizing, human warehousing known as prison, I have been immersed and educated in the arcane workings of police, courts, prosecution and defense, jails and prisons, parole. The inscription over the entrance to Dante's *Inferno* captures the emotional state of those who pass through barred doors: "Abandon hope all you who enter here!"

"You will get the amount of justice you pay for," was the first truism I learned from my attorney. I learned others from observing many of my companions on the "fast track" of justice, as they were zipped along by the three part harmony of overburdened (and often hapless) public defender, prosecutor and judge anxious to clear the docket. One need not be a sociologist to realize the best assets when facing "justice" are to be white and to have money. Behind the razor wire fences, out of sight—and mostly out of mind—incarcerated men and women "do time." Before many days had turned into weeks, my naive middle class assumption that "good guys" wear badges and "bad guys" wear chains had mutated into the realization that the misfits of society wear both. The same must be said of those of noble heart and gentle spirit.

Within these walls I have experienced the most fearful and awful moments of my life, as well as some of the most blessed and awesome. Everyday citizens, whose closest experiences come from television's N.Y.P.D., Judge Judy and the evening news, can never comprehend the deeper realities. Nor do people realize the degree to which their concepts of crime and justice are manipulated by scandal-and tragedy-driven media, or how many unreasoned, knee-jerk laws are rushed into existence in response to polls and for use in the next election's sound bites.

This book is addressed to you, "the People." It is about the systems and institutions which act in your name, and what they do **to** "the least of your brothers and sisters" on your behalf. More important, I offer possibilities and goals for what could be done **for** them instead—and **for** the benefit of victims and communities, at the same time.

This is not a scientifically researched work, but the gleaning of my personal experiences and observations, bolstered by what I have read in many of the resources quoted herein, especially the daily newspapers. While I reference the ways in which crime and the justice systems affect victims and communities, my perspective is that of a prisoner.

By keeping my primary focus on the offenders, I am not wanting either to minimize the harm done to victims and communities, nor to excuse offenders from accountability for their actions. I am, instead, attempting to balance the tableau and broaden the context by inserting the experiences of those most often left out of consideration in the debates concerning the pursuit of justice.

I have been profoundly changed by my proximity to the judicial and penal institutions which act on behalf of "the People." Because of my age, education and theological background, I am able to "stand back" from my immediate situation to sort out and critique the "what, how and why" of it all. It is a sick, broken, rudderless system which neither corrects nor rehabilitates offenders, nor heals or helps victims. It is unworthy of the best of what we are as a people.

Most of my companions lack the verbal or conceptual skills to express their experiences of the brutality and injustices inherent in the "justice" systems. They are more likely to act out their anger and frustrations, both while here, and when they return as your neighbors—as 90% of us will. There is crying need for restorative reforms. For your sake, as well as for theirs—for God's sake—please listen, learn and respond.

A. Companion

*   *   *

It is my hope that this book will effect restorative changes within its readers, that it will be used as a study resource by churches, schools and groups, and ultimately be a contribution toward systemic reforms. To these purposes, I have included discussion starter-guides with each chapter to assist personal or group processing of the material and related issues.

In November 2000, the Catholic Bishops of the United States issued their pastoral letter *Responsibility, Rehabilitation, and Restoration: A Catholic Perspective on Crime and Criminal Justice*. It addresses many of the same issues as this book, and comes to many of the same conclusions. Appendix E (page 156) provides a Cross-Reference between these two resources.

ACKNOWLEDGMENTS

I AM INDEBTED

- to my bishop for his encouragement to write as a continuation of my ministry, and to use my personal experiences of the justice systems and prison to advocate for restorative justice. He has modeled restorative ministry in his care for me.

- to Howard Zehr and his pioneer research and promotion of restorative justice. His universally respected book, *Changing Lenses* (Herald Press, Scottsdale, AZ:1990), has greatly influenced my writing.

- to *The Sacramento Bee*, from which I have drawn much of my data, for its critical, correct and intensive coverage of California's Department of Corrections and prisons.

- to my friends, who have supported my writing by their interest, especially Bob, Estelle, Mike and Suzanne, who reviewed early drafts and made valuable editing contributions.

- to my sister-in-law, Denise, who, by her patient transcription and editing of my handwritten manuscripts, has made this book possible.

PRE-QUIZ

Before reading further, test your present understanding of some of the facts regarding issues of crime, justice and punishment. (See **Appendix A**, page 149, for the answers.)

1) The U.S. Department of Justice estimates the prison population of the United States in 2001 will be:
   a) 230,000   b) 630,000   c) 1,300,000   d) 2,000,000

2) California's "three strikes" law, which mandates a 25 year-to-life sentence, is imposed for:
   a) serious felonies such as murder   b) crimes committed by juveniles
   c) shoplifting and minor drug offenses   d) all of the above

3) A 1994 survey of 157 prison wardens in 8 states asked, "What would be the most effective way to fight crime?" Which response received the highest percentage (71%)?
   a) increase sentences for violent offenders   b) improve public schools
   c) place more police officers on the streets   d) increase job opportunities

4) The rate of incarceration in the U.S. is increasing most rapidly for:
   a) men   b) women   c) about the same

5) Race is an important factor in crime statistics?
   a) yes   b) no   c) can't be determined

6) The percentage of inmates who are functionally illiterate:
   a) 15–25%   b) 25–50%   c) 50–75%   d) 65–80%

7) The 1998 failure rate of parolees (returned to prison) in California?
   a) 15%   b) 25%   c) 45%   d) 75%

8) A state-appointed lawyer representing a California inmate serving a life term at his/her parole board hearing is paid per hour (6 hour maximum):
   a) $24.75   b) $74.25   c) $124.50   d) depends upon crime

9) Race is a major factor in the imposition of the death penalty?
   a) Yes   b) No   c) Applied about proportionally   d) Can't be determined

10) Alternatives to incarceration for non-violent crimes are increasingly being used because of:
       a) prison overcrowding
       b) high recidivism rates
       c) attempts to treat the causes rather than the symptoms of crime
       d) all of the above

Taken from *Peace and Justice Shall Embrace* by A. Companion.
Published by Writers Club Press an imprint of iUniverse.com.

INTRODUCTION

The son of the President of Cyprus had been kidnaped, and his well-being was unknown, as a reporter asked the boy's distraught mother what she hoped would be done to her son's captors when they were apprehended. Her response, "I hope they aren't harmed. I wouldn't want their mothers to suffer what I'm experiencing."[1]

I was a teenager when I heard that interview. It was not the response I had anticipated, nor the one which had spontaneously welled up within me. The profound impact of that woman's amazing compassion in the midst of her own trauma jolted me then, and occasioned my first conscious reflection upon the conflicting feelings of my gut level sense of justice, and my awe at what I had just witnessed.

*   *   *

Almost 40 years later, I was shocked again by an unexpected response to a similar question. It was Respect Life Sunday at our parish, and I had just posed what I intended to be a thought provoking rhetorical question, "Can anyone imagine any situation in which a criminal brought before Jesus for judgment would hear the sentence, 'Crucify him!'?" To my dismay, the source of the defiantly loud, "Yes!," which reverberated throughout the quiet church, was that of my Respect Life Committee coordinator! Once again, that militant response—especially coming from its incongruous source—was not what now seemed so obvious to me. The gospel that Sunday was of the woman caught in adultery who is brought to Jesus in an attempt to trap him into appearing to be "soft on crime."[2] I couldn't keep from smiling as I thought to myself, "That woman was fortunate our 'respect life' coordinator wasn't in the crowd when Jesus invited those without sin to cast the first stone!"

*   *   *

Everyday, in interactions with one another at home, work, in the market place and in the evening news, each of us is confronted with scenarios of real or perceived injustice which invite us to pass sentence and dispense justice. If we are honest with ourselves, few of us are able to boast that our gut level reactions are always in sync with our more lofty professed ideals of justice or the Gospel. We probably hear periodic cries of, "Crucify him!," welling up from our darker inner places, even as we castigate ourselves for not feeling, "There, but for the grace of God, go I," or while saying, "I know that's not very Christian, but…"

Whether we are reading about the atrocities perpetrated by neighbor upon neighbor in the many Rwandas and Bosnias of the world, or are reacting to the hostile driver who has just passed us with horn blaring and middle finger jabbing in our direction, it is the exceptional person whose spontaneous first response is, "Am I also capable of such terrible things?," or "That poor guy must be under a lot of pressure." More often than not, our first visceral reactions to injustices probably more closely mirror that of the respect life coordinator than the mother of the kidnaped boy. Innately oblivious to our own sins, we rush to gather stones.

*   *   *

"Justice" means different things to different people. Philosophers and theologians divide and subdivide it into sundry categories. Merriam-Webster's Collegiate Dictionary's (10th Edition) first definition of justice is, "The maintenance or administration of what is just especially by the impartial adjustment of conflicting claims or the assignment of merited rewards or punishments." It might suffice to imagine the definition Forrest Gump might give us, "Justice is as justice does!"

It is probably fair to say that for the majority of Americans, "justice" has to do with punishment of those who have broken the law, and that "punishment" equates with jail or prison as normative. Historically, America's justice systems function from this mind set, and have the dual goals of determining guilt and punishing the guilty. This is **retributive justice**—inflicting pain for causing pain.

While there has been a gradual evolution toward avoiding what is "cruel and unusual," and toward defining those basic human rights which cannot be denied even the most heinous criminals, most people presume that pain and humiliation are part of the "lesson" which doing justice is supposed to "teach." In reality, that "lesson" easily becomes a contribution to the cycle of violence, rather than a solution to it.

Retributive justice seems to spring from an inherent root within human nature. Anthropologists might connect it to our hunter-warrior ancestors, moral theologians to original sin, psychologists to primal anger. Whatever, we see it manifesting itself in the playpen in retribution for a purloined toy, as well as codified in criminal and civil law.

The ancient Code of Hammurabi (1750 BC) of "an eye for an eye" was a tremendous breakthrough in the evolution of justice, as it promoted the norm of equity in punishment, rather than, "You take out my eye and I'll take out yours—as well as your wife's and children's—and burn your house and village besides!" It held to a vision of human nature as capable of more than our most primitive jungle impulses.

While we have reformed and polished Hammurabi's advancement, and have removed retributive authority from neighbors and placed it in the hands of the state, for the most part it is still "an eye for an eye" which animates both our personal understanding of justice and the state's administration of it.

It could even be argued that the "tough on crime" movement of the past decade and more is a devolution to pre-Hammurabi justice, in which punishments are longer and harsher—often grossly out of proportion to either the seriousness of the crime or its consequences—and are served in brutal and dehumanizing environments. Thirty-seven hundred years after Hammurabi, children as young as 12 are being tried as adults in the United States.

Yet, throughout history, there have been those who have "seen visions and dreamed dreams" of other possibilities, and have believed that the human quest for justice could be imbued with the divine attributes of compassion and mercy, and indeed, that the Divine compels us to "do unto others as you would have them do unto you"—not *as they have done* to you. As Mohandas Gandhi put it, "If an eye for an eye is all there is, soon the whole world will be blind."

In order to be open to new ways of thinking about crime and doing justice, it is crucial to remember that how we define these concepts and our presumptions about them become our self-created "realities." However, retributive justice is only one paradigm. There are other ways. Just as post-Galileo society kept trying to force new data and awareness into the Ptolemaic paradigm of an earth-centered universe—no matter how clearly the new experiences no longer fit the old presumptions—by ignoring what is wrong and dysfunctional in our justice systems, we continue to compound the problems we purport to solve.[3]

In our own time, there is a growing consensus that our present approach to crime and justice isn't working, and that we cannot annually continue to incarcerate a higher and higher percentage of the population. Even if that option were acceptable from humane considerations, it is not affordable for economic ones.

Creative experimental programs are being tried, especially in juvenile justice systems, to develop functioning models of "new visions." In these models, the goals of establishing guilt and setting punishment are maintained, but under the overarching values which guide the process: (1) actively involving victims, offenders and representatives of the community (as well as court officers), (2) in determining an appropriate resolution for this unique situation, (3) which will promote healing, restitution, rehabilitation and reconciliation—peace— for **all** those affected by the crime. This is known as **restorative justice.**

*   *   *

This vision of justice is referred to as "restorative" because it attempts to reestablish personal, relational and community harmony. In promoting harmony (peace), restorative justice flows directly from biblical "dreams and visions," and is supported by Judaeo-Christian principles of social justice and morality. Who has not been stirred by Isaiah's dreams of a time when "the wolf shall be a guest of the lamb" and "swords will be beaten into plowshares?"[4]

Not all crimes can be adequately handled with this approach to establishing justice, nor are all victims and offenders capable of entering into this type of process, but all the systems of adjudication, incarceration, probation and parole are amenable to incorporating restorative principles.

*   *   *

As with "justice," "peace" conjures up various images and definitions. Peace can be the cessation of hostility between warring parties, as well as the enduring condition of peacetime. There is inner peace, which can be both tranquility (freedom from anxiety or fear), and peace with one's self and with God. Even more treasured is the peace which is akin to joy and wholeness which lovers and friends share.

But there is also the peace which parents (and other authority figures) impose by threat of punishment. The political extension of this type of peace is Kosovo—peace only in the most primitive understanding. But peace imposed from the outside is really only suppressed violence. This is equally true whether mandated by court order or patrols of United Nations' peacekeepers. History and human psychology teach us that imposed peace only festers and smolders, eventually manifesting itself in other destructive ways.

There is also an important, but rarely considered, aspect of peace which permeates both our legal and penal systems, and national and international economics and politics. When corporations go to court to seek relief from anti-pollution restraints, or Guatemalan estate owners hire goon squads to intimidate peasants seeking land reform, peace becomes a concept of protecting power or privilege—protection against change, insurance for the status quo.

The flip side of "don't rock the boat" peace is how the status quo is experienced by "the poor," the imprisoned, the powerless and the disenfranchised—as oppression by the same legal systems to which they do not have equal access. It is not "luck" which keeps those with money out of prison, and those without within.

This peace-as-struggle-for-justice is echoed in the dominant biblical concepts and images, which repeatedly proclaim that peace without justice is neither and that the search for one must also be the pursuit of the other. For either to flourish, both must embrace.

Pope Paul VI put it succinctly, "If you wish peace, work for justice." Biblical peace is a spiritual state—a power—which is both a vision and a quest. Biblical peace is manifested in the strength to "conquer evil with good," the patience to "forgive seventy-times seven times," and the memory that "while we were enemies, we were reconciled to God through the death of his son,"[5] not out of our merit, but because of our need.

Biblical justice is concerned with making things right, and with freeing from whatever oppresses people. Biblical justice shows a clear partiality toward the poor and disenfranchised—not because they deserve more, but because they need more in order to experience healing and peace (shalom). "Biblical justice is not measured by the right procedures or the letter of the law having been fulfilled, but by the outcome—have things been made right? The tree is tested by its fruit."[6]

"Shalom is a basic 'core belief' around which many other important beliefs are organized. Shalom encapsulates God's basic intention, God's vision for humankind." Shalom refers to the condition of "all rightness," of things the way they should be. The life, teachings and death of Jesus—the Prince of Peace—were focused on shalom–making.[7]

Just as individuals come to understand that the Holy One is a God of both justice and mercy, and learn to integrate the challenge of "love your neighbor as yourself," so are communities capable of finding ways to balance these values in doing justice and promoting peace.

Just as there seems to be an inborn pull toward "putting out eyes," there is also something "written on our hearts"[8] which calls us toward more noble responses. And when we encounter it at work in others like ourselves, we stand in awe.

*　　　　　　　*　　　　　　　*

Contrasting presumptions—contrasting choices:

Retributive Justice

Crime is a violation of the state, defined by lawbreaking and guilt.
Justice determines blame and administers pain in a contest between the
offender and the state directed by systematic rules.

Restorative Justice

Crime is a violation of people and relationships. It creates obligations to
make things right. Justice involves the victim, the offender, and the
community in a search for solutions which promote repair, reconciliation,
and reassurance.[9]

Restorative justice and spiritually imbued visions of peace are challenging, but doable. The path they chart opens to a fuller humanity and is lined with hope. They offer us measuring tools by which to evaluate and redesign what is, and foundations upon which to build new models which, with the psalmist, proclaim "Peace and justice shall embrace!"[10]

Discussion Guide—Introduction

1) If your child were kidnaped and you had no idea of his/her well-being, how would you respond to the inquiry, "What do you hope will be done to the person who did this to your child?"

2) Can you imagine any situation in which a criminal brought before Jesus for judgment would hear the sentence, "Crucify him!"? Explain the reasons for your response.

3) Recall a personal incident in which you felt an injustice was done to you. Which response most closely resembled yours: "An eye for an eye" or "Swords will be beaten into plowshares"?

4) How would you explain to a 10 year old, "If an eye for an eye is all there is, soon the whole world will be blind?"

5) When you hear or read, "We want to see justice done in this case," what do you understand that to mean?

6) How would you apply, "If you wish peace, work for justice," to a specific local, national or international issue?

Taken from *Peace and Justice Shall Embrace* by A. Companion.
Published by Writers Club Press an imprint of iUniverse.com.

*

*

*

"History demonstrates repeatedly, that, if enough people begin to define themselves as 'good' in contrast to those who are 'bad,' those others come to be seen as less than human…

"I prefer the perspective of the Roman poet Terence, who wrote: 'I am human; I do not think of any thing human as foreign to me.' I feel that it is my business, when I read the news account of some horrible crime, not to regard my 'good' self as completely separated from the 'bad' people depicted in the story but to search my own heart for a connection. I try to see if I understand how it is these people have done what they have done. Not to excuse them, but to draw them closer in order to pray for them and also to pray over what it means to be linked with them in a common humanity."

(Kathleen Norris, *Ama*, NY:Riverhead Books, 1998, p. 176)

*

*

*

I—WHAT SHALL WE DO WITH THE STONES?

One of my fondest memories of growing up in a sparsely populated rural California county is of the evenings spent on my grandfather's lap as we listened to the radio together. Most often, it was the Lone Ranger or the Cisco Kid we shared, as he sculpted thinly sliced apples and offered them to me skewered at the end of his pocket knife. Sometimes, though, I had to endure the news, during which my grandfather—the county brand inspector, who brought many rustlers to justice during his career—commented on the news items. His solutions to the issues of the times were simple, succinct and clear. His answer for just about any kind of crime was, "They ought to take him out and hang him!"

*   *   *

Contemporary to this being written, the bodies of a mother, teenage daughter and another girl have just been found, after disappearing while on a holiday. They had been kidnaped, sexually assaulted and murdered. Today's paper quotes the husband and father of two of the victims as saying, "I believe in capital punishment. And I believe whoever is responsible for this deserves to die. I'll personally pull the switch."

*   *   *

Since my incarceration, I've often wondered if my grandfather would so quickly and dispassionately pass his sentence on me? I can't imagine it. We tend to relate one way to failings of unknown and unseen villains, and another to those we know or love. The former can be dealt with in stereotypes and statistics, but our own kin are "real people" whom we embrace—along with their flaws—in spite of our repulsion. That seems right and natural. Most often family and friendship bonds allow us to find redeeming qualities and mitigating—if not excusing—circumstances to exempt our own from the judgments of those who don't know them. It was easy to empathize with the dilemma in which the brother of the Unabomber found himself, when he discerned his brother to be the long sought, but elusive, killer and maimer.

It is also easy to empathize with the pain and rage of this husband and father as he lashes out at those who so brutally ended not only the lives of his loved ones, but also a part of his. Few of us would be able to resist similar raw emotions, at least as our first response. What complex, conflicting passions would have to be dealt with should the violator also be a loved one, such as a son or brother!

And, when we ourselves are the offenders under attack, every available defense—legal and psychological—is marshaled to defeat or minimize the consequences of justice meted out to us.

When Jesus told the Parable of the Good Samaritan,[1] it was in response to a question of a man "wishing to *justify* (have justice done to) himself," after having been told by Jesus that the path to "eternal life" lies in loving God above all else and one's neighbor as one's self. "And who is my neighbor?" is the jumping off place for Jesus to tell the story of how a man, whose needs were ignored by his own kinsmen, was treated with amazing compassion and generosity by someone he despised, and might well have spat upon as he passed by, had their situations been reversed.

The Good Samaritan story has become part of secular morality, as well as Christian, precisely because it goes against the grain of our biases and instinctual urges, and touches the deeper recesses of our hearts—where the Divine Spirit resides—out of which we wish we could fully live. We stand in awe of the "good Samaritans" we encounter in life, and wish we had what we admire in them.

Jesus tells the story to stretch our understanding of "neighbor" beyond immediate family, racial, religious or national identities—those I know, those I love, those who are like me—to the all-encompassing embrace which is God's. The "truth" of the parable attracts us, but its ramifications, if taken seriously, threaten our awareness of ourselves as "good" and of our society as "just." As with the crowd surrounding the woman caught in adultery, we need to ask Jesus, "What shall we do with the stones?"

*   *   *

One of my first shocks, as I encountered the criminal justice system as a defendant, was hearing the charges against me prefaced by "The People versus…" For the first 55 years of my life, I had considered myself one of the "the people," and now I stood outside of the community defending myself from it, and its desire to do me harm.

Those few, simple words capture the core of our system. Once one enters the courtroom, "*We the People*" mutates into the adversarial, arcane world of "*the* People"—amply represented by prosecutors, bailiffs, clerks, judge and jury—versus the defense attorney, who—for better or worse (the difference more often than not determined by whether you, or "the People" are paying)—stands between you and them.

From now on, neither you nor the plaintiffs will likely have more than cameo appearances in the unfolding drama. This arena belongs to the professional arbiters of the law. Facile as auctioneers, penal code numbers and cultic, archaic phrases—many in Latin to intensify the mysticism—are tossed back and forth between the combatants. And, with the agility of matadors, each side antagonizes, feints and lunges seeking to strike a debilitating blow.

Ostensively, "truth" is the goal to which all players are committed. In reality, each side presents or withholds as much "truth" as seems helpful to winning, and when neither side can hope to prevail by a "preponderance of evidence," the ancillary skills of orator and actor become significant in persuading the jury as to which side holds the copyright to "truth."

When the verdict is reached, the winning side will share congratulatory smiles and handshakes, the losing side will huddle quietly for words of consolation or plans for appeals. The family and friends of accused and accusers will reflect similar reactions. The media will report whether or not the defendant showed any emotion, and will capture a photo of someone's crying mother. If the verdict is guilty, the defendant is hustled out a side door to begin the transition from citizen to convict. Either way, sufficient sheriffs will be on hand to make sure the victorious and vanquished do not continue the quest for justice into the corridors.

*   *   *

In criminal law, crime is defined as an offense against the *state*, not against a person(s). The legal system—not the victims—define both what the crime committed has been, and when justice has been done. The criminal *act* is the crime. The personal and social contexts out of which both victims and offenders come—or in which they are left—are not relevant (unless the *law* defines them as so). Justice is measured by the process: Have the right rules been followed? Then justice has been accomplished.[2]

Just announcing that justice has been done and that it is time to go home (victim, and families and friends of victim and offender), or off to jail (offender) doesn't mean that those most directly affected by the crime have experienced justice, let alone healing or closure. For the most part, their needs and feelings have been shut out of the process.[3]

I have no intention of disparaging the legal profession. I can honestly say, "Some of my best friends are lawyers," and with few exceptions, I would dread facing prosecution in any other country. With all of its defects, American jurisprudence beats most other options. My critique is not of a fatally flawed system, nor those who serve in it, but of the underlying vision and goals which animate it. It is remote, punitive, and lacking in redemptive values.

My experiences as an offender exposed me to both what is noble and unjust in our system, and to people of great integrity and professionalism as well as those who lacked either or both—no different, I suspect, from a cross section of any of our public institutions and those who operate them. No other institution, though, has so much power to impact the lives and futures of those it touches.

My experiences also left me frustrated in several crucial areas. In relationship to those my actions directly injured, I was not allowed—in fact forbidden—to reach out to them in my desire to assist healing, and, if possible, reconciliation. And, in relationship to the larger community, the media—tabloid in bent—became the self-appointed interpreter of events and meanings.

Crime, victims and offenders are all used and manipulated by the media for ratings and by politicians for poll points. What happens to the people most involved is quickly forgotten once the news vans have sped off to the next scandal, and the "tough on crime" news releases have been prepared.

Rather than help facilitate healing and reconciliation, the system keeps victims and offenders apart, requiring them to become adversaries. Rather than facilitate acceptance of responsibility and restitution, the process encourages offenders to deny guilt (or, at least, not to admit it) and to focus on protecting themselves. Reconciliation is not sought because the relationship between victim and offender is not considered important. Except for a formalized pre-sentencing expression of regret, there is no place for repentance—and certainly none for forgiveness.[4]

In my own regard, I accepted my prison sentence as a just consequence of my actions, and with the determination to use the time to as much benefit to myself and others as the limitations allowed. At the same time, I saw it as a terrible waste of talents which could be better used elsewhere as positive and needed contributions to the community. I have not experienced my time in prison so much as punishment, as a waste, although it certainly has contained many losses and painful moments. The victims of my actions are no better off because of my years in prison. I truly hope they have felt some satisfaction that I have been held accountable, but I doubt they are any closer to inner healing now than when we shared separate areas of the courtroom. That hurts me, as well as them.

Nor has my time here benefitted me in any rehabilitative way. Had I not entered prison already educated and skilled, I would have left, as the vast majority of my companions do, as ignorant and incapable of honest economic survival as when I entered. No, I have to take that back. Few leave with as much going for them as when they entered, but return to be your neighbors after years of brutal and dehumanizing warehousing, more angry, more socially inept and more debilitated—not to mention just as addicted or mentally ill. And, since nothing was done to address the factors which contributed to their crimes, most will soon return, to repeat the mean and meaningless cycle once more. (The national recidivism rate average is 60–65%. California's rate was 74% in 1998[5] and 68% in 1999.[6])

Granted the community buys temporary relief by incarcerating drug addicts, the mentally ill, the homeless, repetitive petty criminals and parole violators, along with drug lords, mass murderers and arsonists, but at great costs in both human resources and dollars. At $21,243 per inmate per year, there is a direct connection to crumbling schools, highways and parks. The 1999–2000 budget for California's Department of Corrections was $4,609,000,000.

While there are still very vocal groups actively promoting my grandfather's "one size fits all" remedy for crime, a constantly growing number of penologists, human rights monitors, politicians, religious leaders and "think tanks" are coming to the realization that retribution and human warehousing aren't working. The more enlightened also know they are morally wrong.

The vignettes shared in the following chapter reinforce that conclusion, and show the folly of continuing to pursue the visionless and disparate policies which have created this morass of lost and ineffective systems, which continue to leave in their wake, a trail of broken neighbors needing healing.

*   *   *

"We are a long way from the time when our conscience can be certain of having done everything possible to prevent crime and to control it effectively so that it no longer does harm and, at the same time, to offer to those who commit crimes a way of redeeming themselves and making a positive return to society. If all those in some way involved in the problem tried to…develop this line of thought, perhaps humanity as a whole could take a great step forward in creating a more serene and peaceful society."(Pope John Paul II, July 9, 2000)

Discussion Guide—Chapter I

1) Share an early life experience that helped form your sense of "justice."

2) Respond to the author's assertion that we tend to apply different "rules" of justice and accountability to strangers, than to those of our own family, race or similar lifestyle.

3) Share a "good Samaritan" experience with someone "different" that caused you to rethink or expand your attitude or stereotype of another race, religion or lifestyle.

4) From your perspective, what should be the purposes and goals of incarceration (e.g. juvenile halls, jails, prisons)?

5) Respond to the author's critique of the judicial process.

Taken from *Peace and Justice Shall Embrace* by A. Companion.
Published by Writers Club Press an imprint of iUniverse.com.

II—THROWING STONES

"There is not one man who comes to prison for the first time who is **capable** *of the vast repertoire of crimes he is capable of when he finally gets out of prison. I'm not talking about the fine technicalities of, say, safe-cracking, or the mechanics of murder—No one learns those things in prison…What is forced down their throats in spite of themselves is the* **will** *to commit crimes. It is the* **capability** *I am speaking of." It used to be a pastime of mine to watch the change in men, to observe the blackening of their hearts. It takes place before your eyes. They enter prison more bewildered than afraid. Every step after that, the fear creeps into them. They are experiencing the administration of things no novels or the cinema—not even the worst rumors about prison—can teach. No one is prepared for it." "Even the pigs, when they first start to work in prison, are not prepared for it." "Most important, you learn never to trust a man, even if he seems honest and sincere. You learn how men deceive themselves and how impossible it is to help them without injuring yourself."[1]*

*　　　　　　　　　*　　　　　　　　　*

There is within *each* of us the full potential for whatever good or evil of which humans are capable. What determines which extreme predominates, or which qualities are actuated (or suppressed), depends upon a complex of variables, including genes, mental health, culture, life-experiences, family environment. Without doubt there are people who should never be released from prison, because—no matter the causes, and irrespective of their crimes—they are clearly a constant threat to society. These people make up a very small percentage of those serving life sentences.

Admittedly there is risk involved in trusting in the authenticity of conversion of heart, rehabilitation of lifestyle, and trusting that an education and acquired marketable skills will make a difference. Just as there need to be prudent safeguards when issuing drivers' licenses or allowing free speech, there is justified prudence in setting fair criteria for parole and follow-up supervision. But there are no guarantees with any human being, nor are the lines which separate "us" from "them" all that clear, as is evidenced by the weekly revelations of police and prison guard brutality, corruption of legislators, and convictions reversed because prosecutors withheld exculpatory evidence in order to win.

After two years in prison, a correctional lieutenant asked me what I had learned while here. Among other things, I said, "I've learned that you can't tell the good guys from the bad guys by the uniforms they wear, and that there is just as much corruption among the keepers as among the kept." He didn't disagree, but smiled slightly and responded, "I've often thought that the only thing that separates most of us is that you got caught and we didn't."

When the "keepers"—"the People"—remove themselves too far from the common humanity which they share with the kept, with all its potential for good as well as evil, then "prudence" easily becomes injustice. When the possibility of true rehabilitation is denied, when there is a refusal to consider the unique circumstances and merits of individuals, when incentive to try is taken away, or when hope is killed, a mockery is made of the "justice" system and the meaning of the word itself. What may be just for one person, may not be for another, but no one deserves "blind injustice." Systemic injustice says more about what is wrong with the keepers, than the kept. Even retributive justice needs to say *this* punishment has a defined purpose and a humane goal, and you remain one of us—one of "the People."

*   *   *

"Crime and corrections are at the intersection of rights and responsibilities. Those who commit crimes violate the rights of others and disregard their responsibilities. But the test for the rest of us is whether we will exercise our responsibility to hold the offender accountable without violating his or her rights. Even offenders should be treated with respect for their rights."[2]

Numbers Have Names, Faces and Families

The number of people behind bars in the U.S. grew to a new record of 2 million in 1999, in spite of the slowest prison population growth rate in 20 years in the same year,[3] and in spite of a 10% drop in violent crime in 1999 (the third such drop since 1990). California experienced a 23% drop in violent crime between 1995 and 1998.[4]

One out of every 150 Americans is incarcerated. The number doubled from 1985 to 1998, an annual growth rate of about 6% since 1990: 70% of inmates are illiterate; 10% seriously mentally ill; 60–80% have a long history of substance abuse; the proportion of African Americans arrested for violent crimes has remained steady for 20 years, while the number arrested for drug crimes has tripled; drug related crimes account for 60% of federal prisoners and 23% of state prisoners. Female prisoners are increasing at a faster rate than male (83,000 in this country in 1998), 70% are nonviolent offenders, 75% have children.[5]

California began the year 2000 with 162,000 prisoners, and anticipates having to house 185,865 by 2006. While the number of new inmates is slowing, they are staying longer, due to increased penalties and the expansion of the categories for imposition of "three strikes" sentences under Proposition 21, passed by the voters in March 2000.[6] By April 2001, the state prisons are expected to be at 200% capacity. "By then, we will have exhausted every cranny and nook," says Robert Presley, Cabinet Secretary for prisons. "This is a time to take a critical look at all facets of the correctional system. This is a good time to consider alternatives."[7]

With under 5% of the world's population, the United States has 25% of the world's prison inmates. "It is an important indicator of the sort of society we want to be. We're not only out of step with the rest of the civilized world; this doesn't fit with anything in our own history—or world history." (Jason Ziedenberg, Justice Policy Institute).[8]

The United States currently incarcerates 615 prisoners for every 100,000 of our population. Only Russia exceeds this level, at 690 per 100,000. Most of Europe is under 100. In Asia, rates range from Japan's 36 to Singapore's 229.

"Numbers reflect only a small part of the tragedy, however. Most alarming is the growing disparity in the U.S. prison population. African-American men are imprisoned at a rate six times higher than white men. For African-American women, the rate is seven times higher than for white women…reasons for the prison boom in the United States, most notably our 'drug war' and the conservative crusade that gave us mandatory minimum sentencing laws and 'three strikes you're out' measures."[9]

The drop in crime rates and the increase in incarceration "…leads to a perfectly circular argument by those in the prison-industrial complex: If crime is going down, it's because we've built more prisons—and building even more of them will drive the crime rate even lower."

The prison-industrial complex is a set of bureaucratic, political and economic interests that encourage increased spending on prisons, regardless of actual need. "It is not a conspiracy, it is a confluence of special interests…politicians…areas where prisons have become a cornerstone of economic development…private companies (that reap the $35 billion spent each year on corrections)…government employees (whose jobs and careers depend upon maintaining and expanding prisons). "The prison-industrial complex is a state of mind."[10]

Politics and Profits Pervert Policies

Little of our approach to doing justice is based on the findings of the social sciences, or even the studies commissioned by legislatures, because cliches and TV sound bites fulfill political needs, while the realities of what isn't working threaten the carefully cultivated and choreographed "tough on crime" rhetoric.

"These days, lawmakers are finding great political profit in using the criminal justice system as a flushing ground for those left in the wake of our failed economic and social policies involving drugs, guns, mental illness and impoverished young families. We are pandered to these days with sloganeering ideas like three-strike laws that imprison people for life for minor felony behavior that may not be serious or violent. A community is far more brutalized by habitual use of draconian punishment than by the occurrence of many small crimes."

"These days vengeful laws are destroying a vital component of our criminal justice system, the opportunity for rehabilitation and with it, hope for a future… Without hope, the women and men who appear before me on my morning calendar in criminal court are little more than beasts of prey and I, little more than a hunter."[11]

(Judge Patrick J. Morris, Superior Court of San Bernardino County, CA)

*   *   *

Prior to the 1990 election of Governor Pete Wilson, California's Board of Prison Terms (whose members are appointed by the governor) granted paroles at an average rate of 5% for term-to-life inmates (such as 15-to-life). (Inmates serving determinate sentences are released automatically when their sentences are completed.) (Until 1979, the approval rate was approximately 48%.[12] The board—which has been composed mostly of white, male, former law enforcement officers with no legal training—was instructed by the new governor to close the parole doors. Subsequently, out of over 2,000 annual parole hearings, the board granted release to less than 1%, with only 6 lifers being paroled in 1995 and 9 in 1996.[13]

Surfing the "tough on crime" polls, Governor Gray Davis, who began his term in 1999, pledged to make Wilson seem like a liberal. He campaigned promising "Singapore justice," and he has touted his reversal of all paroles granted by the board to men convicted of non-capital murder as a great victory for public safety.[14] None were paroled in 1999.

"The board and governor have denied paroles for inmates…prison authorities say pose no threat whatever to society, inmates who've maintained unblemished records for years behind bars, who've undergone counseling, earned college degrees, mastered trades and have jobs waiting for them outside. Even when police who arrested them, district attorneys who prosecuted them judges who presided over their trials and—most tellingly—even the victims have urged an inmate's release, the board and governor have denied parole.

"…A mindless parole policy that denies all mercy may provide good copy in a tough-on-crime TV ad in some future presidential run, but it's wrong."[16]

"What we have is a system that has turned an absolutely blind eye to trying to fairly evaluate cases," according to Dennis Kettmeier, a former San Bernardino County district attorney. "They're just saying, well, anybody in for a life term, your parole will be in a pine box."[17]

Just as the governor knows which side of the bread the California Correctional Peace Officers' Association is buttering with its over $2 million contribution to his election, so the board watches the hand which makes and rescinds appointments. This politicizing of what was meant to be a fair, unbiased discernment of merited mitigation of sentences has become a charade in which the outcome is known before the "hearing" begins, and which more and more inmates are refusing to attend. In January 1999, California prisons held 19,519 men and women sentenced to life *with possibility of* parole, but who are denied any such possibility. They have become political prisoners.

State Senator Richard Polanco (D–LA, chair of the Joint Committee on Prison Construction and Operations) called a hearing on April 29, 1999, to probe this politicization. "I'm convinced that we have a process which does not have uniformity and consistency…If we have a justice system, it has to be fair to both the victims and to those who come under our jurisdiction."

Among those testifying for badly needed reforms were former board member Albert Leddy, former California Supreme Court Justice Cruz Reynoso and former U.S. Senator Alan Cranston: "They alleged that board members rudely interrogate inmates and cut off their attorneys; distort facts and refuse to correct mistakes in the record; refuse to acknowledge positive steps toward rehabilitation; ignore letters from prosecutors, judges, prison psychologists and even victim family members urging them to grant parole; and fail to tell inmates what they can do to improve their chances at the next parole hearing.

"They also accused the board of selectively granting parole dates to inmates with political connections, arbitrarily rescinding dates that were previously approved; failing to process appeals in a timely fashion; and violating procedural rules meant to protect inmates' rights."[18]

Testifying before the Assembly Appropriations Committee on August 18, 1999, on behalf of his bill to require fairness and accountability from the Board of Prison Terms, Senator Polanco said:

> "The Penal Code creates a presumption that an inmate will be given a release date, after certain minimum period of incarceration, unless certain findings are made…in practice the opposite is true. In fact, granting a release date is the exception, not the rule. Less than 1% of all life term inmates are given a release date…[the Board of Prison Terms] are rubber-stamping each case—not making any distinctions—treating all inmates like they are Charles Manson.

> "Taxpayers pay for the psychiatrists who evaluate these inmates. Commissioners with no psychology background, routinely ignore these evaluations and make their own determination.

> "This bill is not about early release…does not require the BPT to let people out after a minimum term. This bill is about fairness and uniformity…consistent guidelines, and to look at each case individually, to determine when someone is suitable to be released…The recidivism rate for life-term parolees is about 3% [as compared with about 70% for non-life term felons]…the threat to public safety is very low."[19]

(*SB128 was voted out of committee with a recommendation for approval 14–7.

It was held for future action in anticipation of a probable Davis veto.)

*   *   *

In December 1999, a federal judge ordered the BPT to make sweeping changes in its treatment of prisoners with disabilities, which has included forcing inmates who couldn't walk to crawl up stairs to hearings, keeping shackled the arms of inmates unable to communicate except by sign language, and requiring mentally retarded inmates to sign documents they couldn't read. The judge called the evidence "overwhelming" and "uncontradicted," and said she was "shocked to find that these things occurred with such frequency. More shocking was the level of indifference..."[20]

*   *   *

In March 2000, in reaction to the governor's request for a 7.7% budget increase for the Board of Prison Terms, the State Legislative Analyst responded: "An unwritten policy that effectively ensures that no inmate with a life sentence is released on parole has significant legal, policy and fiscal ramifications for the state criminal justice system. The [BPT] continues to receive full funding for its parole review process despite the current release policy."

The analyst said that in December 1998 there were 16,500 lifers who would—by law—eventually become eligible for parole. Of those, 4,000 are now being held past eligibility at a cost of $100 million annually, and about 500 are added to that number every year to an additional annual cost of $12 million.

The analyst also pointed out those denied parole continue to return for hearings "even though current practice indicates no life-term inmates will be released on parole." This spiraling situation increased the BPT's hearings caseload 140% over the 1990s.[21]

*   *   *

California's 1999–2000 budget included $24 million to begin planning for the State's 34th prison. Another $311 million for construction will come from lease-revenue bonds, which by-pass the need for voter approval or rejection. Interest on the bonds will add $158–300 million more.

The governor had sought $355 million from the budget, but this compromise was struck when "that proposal was blocked by Democratic lawmakers, who argued the State should explore other ways to reduce prisoner overcrowding, such as drug treatment programs or youthful intervention efforts."

Seeking to win over reluctant opponents, Senate President Pro Tem John Burton (D–San Francisco) reminded them that many had voted for the laws which were causing prison overcrowding. Other supporters warned of riots or court ordered releases of prisoners.

The prison, which will hold 2,248 inmates, will take at least two years to construct, during which time at least that many more inmates will have been added to the system which is now nearly at 200% capacity.

Opponents argued the State wouldn't need more prisons if it did more to prevent crime and help inmates reintegrate into society. Of the new prison, Senator John Vasconcellos (D–Santa Clara) said, "It's a dumb, dumb idea…If we were to deal with prisoners constructively, then we wouldn't need a new prison."

As part of the compromise, opponents were able to include the provision that the prison could not open until 3,000 new drug treatment beds are available for inmate rehabilitation programs, and 230 more parole officers are hired.

The "build and incarcerate until we drop" mantra hasn't worked and never can. If the State were to build a new prison every year, the demand for space would still outpace them. Inmate-cynics refer to the politically-hyped "tough on crime" legislation as the "correctional officers' full employment laws." One doesn't have to be an inmate or a cynic to question the relationship between the millions of dollars contributed to political campaigns, and the building-sided push for longer sentences and more prisons by those who benefit from them.[22]

*   *   *

With bulging state prisons and legislators balking at building more, states are turning to privately owned and operated prison companies. By 1998, there was capacity for 13,572 inmates nationally in privately owned prisons.

Congressman Ted Strickland (D–Ohio), a former prison psychologist, has sponsored legislation to prohibit privatization of federal prisons and to limit growth of privately run state prisons. "I find it repugnant that…we are allowing the profit motive to be interjected into our governments' powers of incarceration." "It sickens me to think that individuals sit in corporation board rooms talking about increasing their bottom line when the commodity they are dealing with is captive lives."

"The trend toward prison privatization is disturbing in another way—because of its potentially corrupting effects on public policy. Prison corporations have hired politically well-connected lobbyists to advocate for their cause. The profit motive is also an incentive for private prison advocates to lobby for long-term and mandatory sentences that would keep their beds filled, their profits flowing and their investors happy."[23]

Referring to the "new element in the prison mix: the private, for-profit penal institution," a National Catholic Reporter editorial stated, "How can one expect any sober consideration of prison issues—of reforms or initiatives to reduce prison population—when the prison industry is driven by market forces?"

"What kind of culture quietly tolerates an industry whose growth and success depend on an ever-increasing supply of inmates?

"We've got it all backwards. We are allowing our communities to invest our money in despair and human brokenness. We are feeding profiteers who need society to increase the categories and sentence for which people can be incarcerated."[24]

*   *   *

Prosecutors throughout the country have hid evidence, leading to wrongful convictions, according to a Chicago Tribune analysis of thousands of court records in homicide cases. Since a 1963 U.S. Supreme Court ruling designed to curb misconduct by prosecutors, at least 381 defendants nationwide have had a conviction thrown out because prosecutors concealed evidence suggesting innocence or presented evidence they knew to be false.

"Winning has become more important than doing justice. Nobody runs for Senate saying I did justice."[25]

*   *   *

Over a seven year period in the early 1990s, correctional peace officers at California's Corcoran State Prison killed or wounded 50 inmates, and set up other inmates to compete in gladiator-style fights. When asked to defend the "lackluster state investigation" of these "spectacular abuses," then Attorney General Dan Lungren said that among his challenges were "dealing with the California Correctional Peace Officers' Association," and that "district attorneys in small, rural counties, where many prisons are located, often lack the resources to mount complicated prosecutions…And when DAs do prosecute, sometimes the CCPOA gets even," as the *former* Kings County and the barely reelected Del Norte County district attorneys can testify.

SB451 would have given the attorney general jurisdiction over investigations and prosecutions of alleged abuse by guards when local district attorneys lacked either the resources or the will. The California District Attorneys' Association backed the bill, it was passed by a two-thirds vote in the Senate, and then was killed in the Assembly Public Safety Committee after the "CCPOA heavily lobbied every member of the committee to vote against it."

Attorney General Bill Lockyer actively advocated passage, and explicitly laid out the politics and"how the special interest money game is played." He told the committee, "…it distresses me when unions I respect feel they have to hide the bad apples from public attention." "The Kings County DA got taken out by the CCPOA…there is enormous political risk to even raise this subject in public."

In response to the bill's defeat in committee, Lockyer said, "The odor of special interest cave-in is one I am well qualified to identify." Later, he quoted Assemblyman Jim Battin (who received more that $100,000 from the CCPOA in the prior four years) as saying, "Bill, I'm sorry, but I'm whoring for the CCPOA." Assembly Speaker Pro Tem Fred Keeley asked his colleagues, "If CCPOA weren't in on the play, is there a Democrat who doesn't think this is a good bill?"[26]

*   *   *

The Sixth Amendment to the U.S. Constitution and multiple federal court decisions guarantee the right to effective counsel in criminal cases. Texas is the worst state for flaunting that right. In Texas, each judge decides how much is to be spent on counsel for indigent defendants. In some counties, a maximum of $350 is set even for serious felonies. In a March 1999 survey by the State Bar of Texas, 10% of judges actually admitted favoring lawyers who supported their political campaigns when appointing counsel for indigents, and another 13% said they took that support into consideration.

The ACLU's National Prison Project documents: "Indigent defendants wait in jail for up to six months before a lawyer is appointed to defend them, and longer before they have a chance to first speak with the lawyers."

In June 1999, Gov. George W. Bush vetoed legislation to reform the system, which had unanimously passed both houses of the legislature. According to the director of National Prison Project, the veto continues to assure that "…a lawyer meets his client for the first time 15 minutes before a hearing only to urge the client to plead guilty so the judge can clear his trial calendar and the lawyer can turn a quick profit…a judge demands a campaign contribution from a lawyer in exchange for appointments…"[27]

*   *   *

In a February 2000 interview, Gov. Gray Davis was asked, "What if a judge finds, reasonably finds, that they come to a decision that is contrary to your position?" Davis responded, "They shouldn't be a judge. They should resign. My appointees should reflect my views. They are not there to be independent agents. The are there to reflect what I expressed during the campaign."[28]

Davis went on to say, "Now, they'll either resign or they'll not resign, but they're certainly not going to be elevated, I can assure you of that."

Gerald Uelman, a professor at the Santa Clara University School of Law commented, "I would not appear before any judge he's appointed on a death penalty case without moving to disqualify the judge."

Recalling the governor's earlier insistence that the job of the legislature "is to implement my vision," Senate President Pro Tem John Burton (D–San Francisco) commented, "I think we could abolish state government and let him run it by fiat."[29]

*   *   *

Prior to 1978, nearly one in five condemned prisoners nationwide received commutations to life without parole. Since then, just one out of fifty has.

Historically, clemency has been granted for…having no prior history of violence, those with exemplary behavior in prison, those who sincerely express remorse and those with signs of profound mental illness. It has also been used to rectify sentences dramatically divergent from the sentences of accomplices, or those having committed similar crimes but who were not condemned to death…clemency was instituted to allow for the tempering of justice by considering factors not available to the jury at trial.[30]

But the odds of a governor granting clemency have become more remote…because political considerations have largely overtaken legal argument and appeals to gubernatorial compassion. "Governors just don't do it anymore for fear that clemency grants will be wrapped around their necks at the next election."[31] (Law professor Gerald Uelman, Santa Clara Univ.)

*   *   *

"The fundamental thing the report shows is that the changes in the American prison population are the result of a shift of policy, rather than any basic change in the nature of criminals or the crime rate."

As another indication of how public anger at criminals affected the justice system, the report said that while most crime rates fell beginning in 1991, the proportion of criminals arrested for violent crimes who were sentenced to state prisons jumped sharply…this increase appeared to reflect harsher treatment of criminals by prosecutors, judges and juries.[32]

*   *   *

"There is no area of policy driven more by hysteria, political grandstanding and opportunism than criminal justice." Fearing the political costs of appearing *"soft on crime,"* policy makers opt for *"mindless incarceration…"*[48]
(Jackie Goldberg, Los Angeles City Councilwoman)

Abuse of Power and the Powerlessness of Poverty

"Among themselves, the guards are human. Among themselves, the prisoners are human. Yet between these two the relationship is not human. It is animal. Only in reflection—subjective reflection—do they acknowledge sharing a common consciousness—that we belong to a common species.

*"Prisoners do not make guards what they are. Neither does society in general. The **state** does. It gives them **arbitrary** power over prisoners. They embrace it as a way of life. That is the source of their evil."*[33]

           *   *   *

As of March 2000, the Los Angeles Police Department's Rampart Division scandal has resulted in 29 officers relieved of duty, 70 more under investigation, and over 50 convictions reversed because of planted evidence, fabricated reports, perjured court testimonies and gratuitous violence by police officers. According to former officer Rafael Perez, there was a clique of 30 officers in the anti-gang division that celebrated shootings by awarding plaques to the officers who killed or wounded people.[34] The investigation has led beyond Rampart Division to other areas of the department, as well, and the L.A.P.D. is now being reformed under the supervision of the U. S. Department of Justice.

           *   *   *

Conservative California Republican Assemblyman, Scott Baugh, used to think claims of police brutality and dishonesty were "gross exaggerations." "My view of law enforcement has been profoundly impacted by my own personal experience at the blunt end of a law enforcement stick. To be thrown around in your own home and then have law enforcement deny it—I was flabbergasted, shocked."[35]

           *   *   *

Brutality charges against correctional officers have mushroomed along with the prison population explosion. In the summer of 1998, California's legislature held extensive hearings into allegations of rapes and staged gladiator-style fights set up by officers, as well as unjustified battery and shootings.

Between 1989–1994, more than 30 inmates were shot and killed by prison guards in California—more than the total fatal shootings in all other states and the federal prison system. Investigators testified they were stymied by a code of silence among prison guards. Whistle blowers said they faced retaliation from their superiors.

"Basically, there's been a reign of death. We must recognize a clear and compelling pattern of awful events—little reported, barely investigated, mostly exonerated, little sanctioned."(Sen. John Vasconcellos, D–Santa Clara)

While training for guards was found to be woefully inadequate, Sen. Ruben Ayala, D–Rancho Cucamonga, questioned whether training was enough. "How many weeks of training would it take for a guard to learn not to us a Taser on an inmate's testicles, or that you don't smash an inmate's head into a window?"[36]

*   *   *

In late 1999, investigations into alleged sexual harassment and assault by male guards were begun at all four California prisons for women. One woman alleges her child was fathered by a prison staffer; others that they spent their sentences fending off sexual advances from guards and work crew supervisors.

In October, the head medical officer at Valley State Prison was reassigned to a desk job in Sacramento, after explaining on a network news program that his staff gave pelvic exams to women inmates complaining of headaches, because "it's the only male contact they get," and that they enjoyed it.[37]

*   *   *

In 1980, there was only one "supermax" prison in the United States. Today, there are more than 50. Forty-two states, the District of Columbia and the federal Bureau of Prisons each have at least one. The terms differ for these "control units," but these conditions are common to all: 22-to 23-hours-a-day solitary lockdown, solitary meals and recreation, severely restricted access to work opportunities, social services and religious services.

The degree of deprivation varies, but human contact is kept to a severe minimum. Windowless cells and thick steel doors and walls prohibit intra-cell communication. Many facilities deny access to sunshine. Meals and Holy Communion come through the slot in the door. Visits with loved ones are through plexiglass windows and monitored by guards.

Whereas, "control units" were once limited to the "worst of the worst," today they are commonly used for behavior modification and social control, rather than for security purposes. In Europe, the use of such units is extremely small and for very restricted circumstances. In February 2000, New York-based Human Rights Watch wrote: "Prolonged segregation that previously would have been deemed extraordinary and inconsistent with concepts of dignity, humanity and decency has become a corrections staple." In both Texas and California, 7% of inmates are housed in "control units," a two-fold increase from five years ago.

"Stuart Grassien, a Harvard Medical School psychiatrist and one of the country's leading specialists on the mental effects of solitary confinement, said that it is 'toxic to mental functioning.' Under prolonged solitary confinement, the mentally ill become sicker and the psychologically healthy show signs of acute mental illness. The psychological damage is akin to that suffered by torture victims, prisoners of war and Arctic explorers…two key functions of the mind are affected: the ability to focus attention and the ability to shift attention…'you are in a mental fog."

Recognizing the damage the psychological damage that can be done by prolonged isolation and social deprivation, the 1959 Manual of Standards of the American Correctional

Association recommended a "few days" for minor infractions and "30 to 90 days in extraordinary circumstances." Today, though, no clear guidelines exist, and who is confined, for what, and for how long is often at the discretion or whim of prison officials. It is not unusual for "supermax" confinement to continue for months, or even years.[38]

*   *   *

Amnesty International placed the United States on its 1999 list of human rights violators, in the company of Algeria, Cambodia and Turkey, among others, because of police brutality, violations against people in detention and increased numbers of executions (78 in 1998).

"Human rights violations in the United States are persistent, widespread and appear to disproportionately affect people of racial and ethnic minority backgrounds."[39]

*   *   *

Comedian Richard Pryor knowingly jokes that when blacks go to court looking for justice, "that's what we find: just us."

U.S. Supreme Court Justice Sandra Day O'Connor knows it is no joke: "We have a good many citizens in this country who think justice is just for us, the privileged few at Stanford, the upper class, but not for them. Many African-American citizens think the system operates unfairly...we have some work to do."[40]

"In our adversary system of criminal justice, a person hauled into court who is too poor to hire a lawyer cannot be assured a fair trial unless counsel is provided for him...lawyers in criminal cases are necessities, not luxuries." (U.S. Supreme Court, 1963)

"We are more casual about qualifying the people we allow to act as advocates in the courtrooms than we are about licensing our electricians." (Chief Justice Warren Burger)

"What it boils down to is you get what you pay for. Look who's on a court appointed list anywhere. Very few experienced lawyers are on those lists, and the reason is, they can't afford to be on them.

"So you either have inexperienced attorneys right out of law school for whom any money is better than no money. Or you have people who are really bad lawyers who can't make a living except off the court appointed list...I don't think it serves justice."

Public defenders are usually crushingly overburdened with cases and unable to give the needed time and attention.[41]

*   *   *

State appointed attorneys representing indigent inmates at California parole board hearings receive $23.75 per hour, with a six hour maximum ($142.50) per client. The scales of justice are heavily weighted against the poor.

Mandatory-Minimums and Three-Strike Sentences Create Injustices

My friend Curtis is serving 50 years-to-life on a fourth strike conviction. Three of Curtis' convictions were drug induced crimes: two for robberies totaling less that $150 while high on cocaine, one for possession for less than $20 worth of cocaine. The fourth was a false conviction for a robbery for which he had neither any remote involvement, nor a competent public defender. Curtis did not sell drugs, no one was ever threatened or hurt, no property was damaged, no weapon was used. Curtis had a drug addiction problem. He was and is a danger to no one. He is now 37, a born again Christian who may well die in prison. When new regulations requiring inmates with more than 20 years to serve caused Curtis to be transferred to a maximum security prison, even jaded staff cried.

While Curtis is a particularly egregious example of three-strikes gone awry, his is not a rare situation.

In 1998, the California Supreme Court upheld a 25-years-to-life sentence for a man convicted under the three-strikes for shoplifting a carton of cigarettes. Fifteen years earlier, he had been convicted of attempted murder during a burglary.

The ruling evoked an editorial in The Sacramento Bee entitled "Sledgehammer Justice." "…this ruling illustrates the most troubling flaw in three-strikes law. Under it, a minor crime committed decades later—after years in which a criminal defendant may have led an exemplary crime-free life—can lead to life imprisonment.

"That's wrong. It not only wastes valuable and expensive prison space, it's unjust. Should anyone spend life in prison for shoplifting a carton of cigarettes?"[42]

In February 1999, another man received the same sentence for "felony evasion" (running from the police while under the influence of methamphetamine). He was on parole and had two prior convictions from the 1980s.

At a rally shortly afterwards calling for revision of three-strikes to limit its draconian sentences to violent and serious felonies, Orange County Superior Court Judge James P. Gray (a former prosecutor) said, "We have to bring some reason to the debate, not just emotion. Every time a congressman's child gets caught with drugs, they want treatment for him. Every time someone else's child gets caught, they want prison for them."

Prosecutors and judges in Orange, Los Angeles and San Diego Counties apply three-strikes more frequently than other counties, yet studies show no greater decrease in crime than in counties which use it less aggressively. San Francisco, which applies three-strikes most sparingly in the state, has seen a greater decline in crime than any of the three southern counties.[43]

*   *   *

In February 2000, two Placer County (CA) jurors balked at sending a bicycle thief to prison for life. Joe Wilcox told the judge, "Your Honor, I have a moral objection to being part of a process that would impose a life sentence on someone for stealing a $300 bike." Fellow juror Debbie Holland added, "Morally, I can't do it either." The judge dismissed them and replaced them with alternates.

Commenting on what happened, "three strikes" critic, State Senator John Vasconcellos (D–Santa Clara) said, "I expect that to grow. Anyone with an active moral compass couldn't be a party to sending someone to life in prison over $300. Gradually, it will dawn on people to the change the law."[44]

*   *   *

California's three-strikes law is the severest in the nation. The other 24 states with three-strikes laws limit life sentences to serious and violent felonies. In California, half of those serving 25-to-life terms are doing so for crimes such as drug possession, petty theft, burglary and writing bad checks. "Housing these convicts, most between 25 and 34 years old, for the rest of their lives poses a colossal drain on tax revenues and a huge waste of lives."[45]

At the end of September 1999, about 33,800 inmates were in California prisons with a second strike, and about 5,700 with a third strike. The annual increase has been steady since 1996. The Department of Corrections estimates that by 2005 there will be 38,000 second-strikers and 12,000 third-strikers, making up 28% of the prison population, in contrast to 22% now.[46]

State Senator Tom Hayden (D–LA) attempted to revise the law to apply only to violent and serious crimes (SB79), but has postponed a vote on his bill until the next legislative session, fearing it might not pass the senate, and certainly would be vetoed by the governor, who vetoed a bill which would simply have studied the effects of three-strikes and made recommendations. The California Three Strikes Project Political Action Committee is now beginning the process of trying to bring the issue to a vote of the electorate through a ballot initiative.[47]

A University of California, Berkeley, study, released in November 1999, concluded there is "no statistical evidence that the law has contributed to an overall drop in crimes." "The study found that before the law took effect [1994], persons with one or two strikes on their record were responsible for 13.9% of all adult felony arrests in [Los Angeles, San Diego, San Francisco]. But after 'three strikes'…the number fell only slightly to 12.8% of arrests."

The study concluded, "There is a large gap between the substantial declines in crime in California that started in 1991 and have continued to 1999 and the detectable impact of 'three strikes'."[48]

Political commentator, Dan Walters, reacted to the study: "Whether true or not, the UC study's conclusions are irrelevant. The only thing that counts is that the three strikes law is popular...[the approach to this issue has] "little, if any, relationship to fact or logic." [Three strikes has become] "a political third rail that could electrocute any politician bold or foolish enough to touch it."[49]

Mandatory-minimum sentencing laws are the primary reason for burgeoning prison populations. While some discretion is sometimes allowed, judges are forced to impose designated sentences regardless of the obvious and blunt injustices inflicted.

A recent Gallup Poll found that 90% of the 350 state and 49 federal judges polled opposed federal mandatory minimum sentencing for drug offenses.

Referring to California's "three-strikes" law, Sacramento County Superior Court Judge Barry Loncke says sentencing criteria "are so warped these days because of the political need to satisfy a public that seems unaware of the consequences of these mandatory-minimum schemes." Referring to the statistics that more than half of those being sentenced to 25-to-life are minorities, Judge Loncke said, "Our laws are having the effect of genocide. Prisons are, in fact, becoming concentration camps for a group of people who don't need to be there."[50]

In Victor Hugo's *Les Miserables* (popularized by the musical of the same name), "the People" (personified by law-blinded Detective Javert) pursue Jean Valjean for 19 years for the crime of breaking a window and taking a loaf of bread to feed his starving niece. Justice has to have more meaning than this.

Marc Klaas, father of Polly Klaas (the 12-year-old Petaluma, California, girl kidnaped from her home and murdered) promoted California's "three strikes and you're out law." Now after seeing its effects, he is working to change it. Three strikes means "you can get life for breaking into someone's garage and stealing a stereo. I've had my stereo stolen, and I've had my daughter stolen. I believe I know the difference."[51] Polly's 80-year-old grandfather, Jack Klaas adds, "To take someone who has committed a nonviolent crime and send them to prison for 25 years to life is unconscionable. To have [Polly's] name used to perpetuate this fraud on the people of California I think is a disgrace."[52]

Criminologists still debate the causal relationship between three-strikes[x] and the drop in

---

x Under "three strikes," previously committed serious or violent felonies are "strikes." With one strike, conviction for any new felony requires double the normal sentence; with two strikes, *any* new conviction requires a *minimum* of 25-years-to-life.

the crime rate. Yet, obviously, it has removed many habitual and dangerous criminals from the streets for long periods. I even support the goal of three-strikes. But, like the controversial drift nets which indiscriminately sweep the oceans scooping up anything that swims, along with the sought after marketable fish, three-strikes lacks the discernment mechanisms for separating habitual, violent criminals from those who have committed isolated crimes—there is a big difference.

Build Treatment Programs, Not Prisons

"At least once a week during the month before they were locked up, 69% of federal prisoners, 76% of state prisoners and 70% of jail inmates used drugs."

"Illegal drugs and alcohol helped lead to imprisonment of four out of five inmates," according to a three-year-study by the National Center on Addiction and Substance Abuse at Columbia University. According to the report, "Behind Bars," 1.4 million of the 1.7 million prisoners in 1996 "had violated drug or alcohol laws, had been high when they committed their crimes, had stolen to support their habit or had a history of drug and alcohol abuse that led them to commit crimes.

"But while 840,000 federal and state prisoners needed drug treatment in 1996…fewer than 150,000 received any care before being released."

Joseph Califano, Jr., director of the center and former secretary of the U.S. Dept. of Health and Human Services, said, "The most troublesome aspect of these grim statistics is that the nation is doing so little to change them," and that long mandatory sentences for addicted felons "makes no sense" because it removes the incentive to get treatment in order to get out of prison, and simply returns those most likely to reoffend back into society.[53]

Mandatory-minimums have been used as a major weapon in the "war on drugs." As a result, it is now common to get a longer sentence for selling a joint of marijuana to a neighbor than for sexually abusing her.

Former Michigan Governor William Milliken called signing the "650 Lifer Law" his biggest mistake. The 1978 law mandated life-without-parole for possession of 650g heroin or cocaine with intention to sell it. The goal was to catch major drug dealers. The result, though: 86% were first time offenders, 70% poor, mostly young people. (The law was modified in 1998 allowing parole after 15 years.)

In 1995, Utah eliminated mandatory-minimums for certain crimes and situations. By contrast, 80% of second-time drug offenders serving life sentences in Georgia were convicted of selling less that $50 worth of drugs.[54]

Women convicted of drug crimes often serve longer sentences than their boyfriends, who are usually responsible for their involvement. The reasons are that the boyfriends can name names and arrange plea bargains for lesser sentences. The women either don't know enough to have any information to trade, or they simply refuse to snitch on loved ones or family members, or to cooperate by wearing wiretaps or going undercover.[55]

In 1986, Congress passed mandatory sentencing laws requiring an automatic five-year prison term for federal convictions of possession of as little as 5 grams of *crack* cocaine. This applies even to first time offenders. Three hundred people are being incarcerated under this law every month—84% of them black.

Those convicted of possession of 5 grams of cocaine in *powder form* will likely receive probation. It takes 500 grams of powder cocaine before the five-year mandatory sentence kicks in. The vast majority of those convicted of powder cocaine possession are white.[56]

*   *   *

While the federal government spends only 20% of its $17 billion drug-control budget to treat addicts, a new study by Physician Leadership on National Drug Policy shows medical treatment works, reduces crime and is much cheaper than incarceration. Annual approximate costs per person:

> Incarceration $25,000, long-term residential treatment $6,800,
> short-term residential treatment $4,400, methadone maintenance $3,900,
> intensive outpatient care $2,500, regular outpatient care $1,800.[57]

*   *   *

A report by the California Legislative Analyst's Office recommends the state spend twice as much on alcohol and drug treatment programs.

At the end of 1998, the state's 1,800 licensed treatment programs had room for 70,000 adults (almost no publicly funded residential treatment is available for adolescents). Counties had waiting lists totaling 5,000 more, and estimated 56,000 others would seek treatment if it were available. It would cost an additional $63 million to treat those on the waiting lists, and $330 million more to reach the others.

Sacramento County reports nearly 80% of arrests and child protective services involve substance abuse. The analyst's report says "many studies show drug treatment is cost-effective for society in terms of reduced criminality, medical and welfare costs."[58]

*   *   *

In July 1999, Governor Gray Davis vetoed AB 1112 by Assemblyman Rod Wright (D–Los Angeles). The bill would have shifted some low-risk inmates and parole violators into community-based programs of "intermediate sanctions," rather than keeping them in prison. The bill would have set up experimental programs in at least two counties, and envisioned drug treatment, counseling, daytime check-in centers and home detention with electronic monitoring.

"If this was a decision solely based on what is good policy, the governor would have signed it. The problem is the crime issue right now is owned by the prison guard's union. This is all about politics," commented Dan Macallair of the Center on Juvenile Crime and Justice in San Francisco.[59]

Treatment, Not Imprisonment, for Mentally Ill

I watched with aching heart as four officers came to take Charlie off the tier. Charlie hears voices and argues with them, he also likes to play loud rap music and to sing and dance along. Both things brought constant complaints and harassment from both the men around him and the officers. On the occasions when the music disturbed me, I would quietly ask him to turn it down, which he always did immediately and with great apology. In between times, I'd sometimes surprise him with candy or a soup, and go out of my way to greet him on the yard, where he was always alone with his radio. One day I said, "How's it going, Charlie?" He responded with a big grin, "You're a very patient man." That made my day and cemented a bond between us.

It hurt to listen to the officers all yelling conflicting directions at the same time, and to Charlie's terrified pleas, "What did I do wrong? How do I know you aren't going to kill me? Please, I'll be good!" Then I watched as Charlie was led away in handcuffs, tears streaming down his face, scared, alone and defeated again.

I don't know what Charlie did to be imprisoned, but the real crime is that this is the best "the People" can do for him.

* * *

Duane Silva (IQ of 70—the mental capacity of a 10 year old) was one of the first victims of California's "three-strikes" law. Now 25, he is serving 28-to-life for stealing a VCR and some jewelry in a residential burglary. His previous strikes were for arson: the first when he set fire to a trash can, the second when a fire began in a truck where he had been playing with matches.[60]

* * *

Los Angeles County Jail is, by default, the nation's largest mental hospital. On an average day, it holds 1,500 to 1,700 inmates who are severely mentally ill, most held for minor offenses, such as being a public nuisance.[61]

California spends $700 million annually to incarcerate and treat 19,000 mentally ill inmates. The State judicial system spends $1.2–1.8 million each year arresting, prosecuting and jailing mentally ill persons (most of whom were not receiving mental health treatment prior to their arrest).[62]

*   *   *

In August 1998, the California Department of Corrections conceded liability and settled a class-action suit brought on behalf of the 5,000 prisoners with mental retardation, autism, cerebral palsy and other developmental disabilities. The suit charged that guards throughout the system taunted and punished developmentally disabled inmates who could not understand prison rules, walk or speak quickly enough or ask for help when hurt or sick. Disabled prisoners have been denied prison jobs and parole because they could not learn needed skills in general population classes, and they have been left to be preyed upon by predatory inmates.[63]

*   *   *

The first comprehensive, nationwide survey of incarcerated mentally ill inmates was released by the U.S. Dept. of Justice in July 1999. "The report confirms the belief of many state, local and federal experts that jails and prisons have become the nation's new mental hospitals." The study concluded that at least 16% of the total inmate population suffer from mental illness.

The study details how "emotionally disturbed inmates tend to follow a revolving door from homelessness to incarceration then back to the streets without treatment, many of them arrested for crimes that grow out of their mental illnesses…bizarre public behavior, or petty crimes like loitering or public intoxication." Those in state prisons "were more likely than other prisoners to have been convicted of a violent crime," and to "spend an average of 15 months longer behind bars than other prisoners, often because their delusions, hallucinations or paranoia make them more likely to get into fights or receive disciplinary reports."

"With the wholesale closing of mental hospitals in the 1960s…many states failed to build a promised network of clinics to monitor patients." The prison boom of the past two decades took up the slack. "Jails have become the poor person's mental hospitals."[64]

The Sick and the Senile

"Picture an 86-year-old-man clutching a walker as he shuffles down a prison hallway…in frail health, severely depressed and a threat to no one." John Bedarka was sentenced to life without parole for shooting his wife's lover over 30 years ago.

"With three-strikes laws becoming common and some states abolishing parole altogether, the ranks of these aging, sickly inmates will only keep growing—as well as the costs to taxpayers" (at a rate of about three times more, or $65,000 per inmate).

Pennsylvania staffs an 85 bed long-term-care unit with 48 nurses around the clock. The demand for more beds is leading to a $23 million expansion to triple the number of beds.[65] Other states are caught in the same bind. California's corrections chief, Robert Presley, is considering a "geriatric prison" built for elderly inmates, with wheelchair ramps and on site nursing care. California now has 5,000 inmates over age 55 and the number will continue to increase.[66]

In 1998, The U.S. Supreme Court ruled that prisons and jails are covered by the Americans With Disabilities Act of 1990. This means that prisoners with disabilities (including chronic diseases) are entitled to appropriate treatments, facilities and programs.

The recidivism rate of parolees over 50 is 4%; after 60, less than 1%. Besides the political issues involved with releasing any inmate, elderly inmates—especially sick ones—face even more daunting problems returning to society after years of debilitating dependency. Nothing in prison prepares them for returning, and few communities are prepared to provide the support services needed to receive them.[67]

California's over-50 prisoner population rose from less that 1% to 2.7% over the past 10 years. It is expected to be 8% by 2025. Preparing to care for elderly inmates needing geriatric and chronic illness care will cost additional millions.[68]

"We are constantly faced with low-risk, high-cost prisoners who should be moved into some kind of supervised release…But there is no infrastructure in most states to accept large numbers of released older prisoners," says Jonathan Turley, founder of George Washington University's Project for Older Prisoners, which helps win parole and community placements for elderly inmates. He argues that states could reap tremendous savings by investing a fraction of their corrections' budget into a post-prison alternative.[69]

Sr. Helen Prejean, CSJ, author of *Dead Man Walking*, speaks of "the feeling of death that grips the hearts of prisoners who face years behind bars. The feeling is intensified by the degrading conditions and treatment they encounter, which conveys a message, 'You're nothing but human waste.'" The suicide rate of inmates is nine times higher than the national average. AIDS is the second leading cause of death among inmates. "With the low levels of palliative care that are available in most prison infirmaries…and the reluctance of prison doctors to administer analgesics, especially narcotics, many die alone and in pain, far from family and friends who could have provided caring support had they been released."[70]

*   *   *

A few months ago, I attended a memorial service in the prison chapel for a man I knew only in passing. I don't know why John was in prison, nor do I know much about his background, except that he was a biker and that he had been married five times. The John I knew was past 70, racked with cancer, and shuffling inch by inch in excruciating pain supported by his aluminum walker and one of his much younger biker brothers. John was a walking petition for mercy and for letting go of vengeance.

John was also an indictment of a system—of a society—bent on the extraction of the last ounce of flesh, of owning the last gasp and heartbeat of a dying and broken man in the name of "justice." John died alone in the prison hospital cut off from his biker buddies and whatever family he may have had. "The People" were diminished and something of "justice" died, too.

What great victory for "justice" is served by keeping sick, broken, nonviolent men in prison?

13-Year-Old "Adults"

As we begin the 21st Century, can you name the only countries known to still execute juvenile offenders? You may have correctly guessed Iran, Saudi Arabia, Pakistan and Yemen, but, if you left out the United States you would have missed the country with the most such executions. More than two dozen of the death row inmates in Texas are juveniles—an estimated 10% of them are mentally retarded.[71]

In July 1899, Illinois established the first juvenile court in the nation, becoming the first state to codify the mounting research which clearly showed that children were developmentally different from adults, and should not be treated simply as "small adults" before the law. The goals of the juvenile court systems which have since evolved have been intervention and rehabilitation.

Florida and New York have led the national reversion to more medieval approaches to juvenile crime. In the past 15 years, since Florida pioneered giving prosecutors (rather than judges) the discretion to try juveniles as adults, the numbers of children incarcerated in adult prisons have risen 200%.

In New York, any 14-year-old arrested for a violent crime is automatically tried as an adult; any 16-year-old arrested for any felony faces adult prosecution. Many states allow 13-year-olds to be tried and sentenced as adults for first-degree murder. In 24 states, 16-year-olds can be sentenced to death.[72]

In March 1999, the "Juvenile Justice Initiative" was passed by "the People" of California. It expands the number of offenses for which a child as young as 14 can be tried as an adult [the minimum age in California was 16] and gives to district attorneys the authority judges had to determine if a juvenile will be tried as an adult. There are no provisions for intervention to reach troubled youth before they turn to criminal activity, nor any rehabilitative components.[73] This harsher stand comes even though California's rate of juvenile arrests for violent crime has fallen even faster than the national average since 1995 (CA–38.8%; US–23.8%).[74]

The growing trend of prosecuting juveniles as adults consigns the youths to prisons, rather than crucial rehabilitative services at their still malleable age. In December 1999, California adult prisons held 117 minors aged 16 or 17. The State Legislative Analyst estimates it would cost $300 million to construct new, separate housing for minors.[75] It is well established that youths placed in the prison system are far more likely to continue down the path of violent criminality as adults, and that they are far more likely to be raped or to commit suicide than their adult counterparts.[76]

*   *   *

A study by the Justice Policy Institute (San Francisco, February 2000) reported that "Minority youths arrested on violent felony charges in California are more than twice as likely as their white counterparts to be transferred out of the juvenile-justice system and tried as adults…Once they are in adult courts, young black offenders are 18 times more likely to be jailed—and Hispanics 7 times more likely—than are young white offenders."

"Over the past six years, 43 states have passed laws that make it easier to try juveniles as adults. In Texas and Connecticut in 1996, the last year for which statistics are available, all the juveniles in jails were minorities."[77]

*   *   *

A scathing state inspector general's report (1999) on Ventura School, the only CYA facility for women, said that female wards and staff live in a "climate of fear and suspicion," as a result of alleged sexual exploitation and "code of silence" by staff.[78]

"CYA has moved far from its origins as a reform institution dedicated to the rehabilitation of young criminals. It now increasingly resembles an ordinary prison system, with lockups every bit as brutal as any adult prison in the state. A six-month investigation into allegations of misconduct at the CYA's Herman G. Stark Youth Correctional Facility in Chino found evidence of wards being slammed against walls, forcibly drugged, confined in cells soiled by urine and feces and deliberately set up by staff for fights with other wards."

Of the more than 7,500 CYA wards, 2,000 cannot get needed drug treatment, 700 are unable to get treatment for severe psychological disabilities or sexual deviancy. Only half of the 1,300 wards at Chino even attend school.[79]

Doing Time—Wasting Time

In a candid moment of frustration, my prison vocational instructor confided, "All the Department of Corrections expects of me is that I take roll and turn in my reports on time. Anything else is on me." It was not difficult to discern the low priority the education and vocational programs have when I discovered (in 1999) that my *Introduction to Computers* text had been printed in 1985, and the classroom was a former storage room bereft of heat or air conditioning, with a learning environment temperature range from the mid-50s to 100° F. The class program development budget for the year was $360.

As I write, my cellie is preparing for a state certification exam in automobile transmissions. His class hasn't met for a month, so he has barely seen or touched an actual transmission. He and two other men coordinate their study schedules since they have to share the only manual—one which doesn't include the technological changes of the past five years.

Most citizens probably presume, as I did, that an effort is made to rehabilitate prisoners, with the hope they will one day return to society as productive citizens. The truth is that the designation "Department of Corrections" is an Orwellian parody in itself. Prison neither "corrects" nor rehabilitates, nor does it make any meaningful effort to do so. By political mandate, California prisons are simply warehouses of human potential, graveyards for the human spirit. In the manner of the great black holes of outer space—by their very nature and design—they suck out what is good, hopeful and humane from the inner space of those committed to their custody.

Approximately two-thirds of inmates are illiterate, or only able to read and write at a very basic level.[80] Most inmates enter the system as teens or even younger. They grow up physically while incarcerated, but their social, psychological and emotional development fixate at a primitive level. Prison life becomes normative, prison values and mores become theirs, the "homies" become family.

While the physical facilities of each prison differ somewhat, the basic environment and lifestyle are similar. Not much distinguishes one day from another: the schedule is the same, the menus predictable, the scenery never changes. The routine creates a rhythm of order, as well as monotony. For those not in school, without a job or unable to read, the hours are filled by TV, physical exercise and hanging out. Many inmates become so institutionalized they become incapable of functioning anywhere else.

*   *   *

"For people in prison, literacy is more than just an educational issue; there's a direct correlation between the ability to read and write and public safety. Studies in Illinois, Florida, Alabama and New York found that adult inmates engaged in academic education had lower criminal involvement, less recidivism, higher employment and more likelihood of continuing their education once they were released. The more education people have and the more literate they become, the less likely they are to commit crimes."[81]

*   *   *

In 1994, Congress ended the use of Pell grants for higher education for prisoners, despite studies showing that education has been proven to be one of the most effective means of reducing recidivism. Funding for educational and vocational programs continues to decline as the prison population grows and budgets are weighted more and more to cover custody requirements. The quality of what remains deteriorates; the waiting lists to enter programs grow. Instead of making every effort to prepare inmates for eventual reentry into the community, programs to do so are being cut or underfunded.

"CDC statistics show barely half of all prison inmates participating in programs at any given time and less than a quarter receiving the kind of education and vocational training that might enable them to get a job and integrate into the community."

"A number of factors account for the small percentage of inmates participating in programs. Foremost among these is the fundamental belief of the State's correctional officials that the behavior of most prison inmates cannot be changed. The Secretary of the Youth and Adult Corrections Agency told the Commission: 'The Department of Corrections' mission is to house the felons who are convicted and sent to prison. The mission is not to "correct" them. Our mission is to provide the sanction that the courts imposed…corrections is really derived from the principle of correcting the conduct by taking them out of law-abiding society.'"[82]

The Parody of Parole

Lewis left prison in mid-November 1997 with the clothes he was wearing and the $200 given to all prisoners as they walk out the gate. He had to report to his parole officer the next day. When he arrived, his gate money had been diminished by Greyhound fare, first night's lodging and meals. He had no one waiting for him, no place to live, no job. He found a boarding house which took in men with alcohol and drug problem backgrounds. He shared a room with three other men and had use of a common kitchen for $200 a month. His first monthly general assistance check of $214 would arrive five weeks later.

*   *   *

What private corporation could consistently produce a 65–75% failure rate[83] in its products without a stockholder revolt? California taxpayers need to know that their prison and parole systems are failures. The system's "graduates" return to the streets without social or economic skills, or the transitional support to make it. The system presumes they will fail, sets them up for failure, then punishes them again for failing.

"California taxpayers spend $245 million a year to monitor 100,000 newly released inmates…When parolees fail, taxpayers spend another $1.5 billion to return them to prison and maintain them there.

"It's money that would be better spent [as the legislative Analyst's Office recommends] on housing, drug and alcohol counseling and job help programs to assist ex-cons, many of whom are mentally and socially fragile, to live productive, crime-free lives.

"Sadly, California invests almost nothing to reduce parolee failure…some 80,000 parolees are unemployed, but the parole system offers no job help for most of them; 85,000 are alcoholics or drug addicts, but the system has only 750 treatment beds; an estimated 10,000 are homeless, but there's shelter space for just 200…"

"…Money spent to help former criminals conquer their drug and alcohol addictions, get jobs and lead stable lives is cost effective crime prevention."[84]

*   *   *

"Since 1995 the [Board of Prison Terms] has tightened its parole revocation policies to the point that 53 percent of all state prisoners in 1999 came into the system for violating the terms of their release. In 1993, by comparison, that figure was 35 percent."[85]

"…adequate attention—education, drug treatment, job skills—is not given to the more than 50,000 inmates who complete their terms each year. One minute behind electric fences, the next minute at the bus depot. Most of them end up back in prison in a matter of months—nearly half of them convicted of a new crime.

"The cost of failure is high. Under recently enacted laws, repeat felons receive longer terms. As a result of the longer sentences, they are considered dangerous and are restricted to costly, high-security prisons—further committing the State to the most expensive tool in the corrections arsenal."[86]

*   *   *

Instead of providing a helping hand up and out, in June 1998, the Department of Corrections announced a new, more punitive approach to "teach" parole violators. Pilot programs at three prisons will assign parole violators to intense manual labor without pay. They will be denied family visits and packages from home. Phone calls will be allowed only for "emergencies." CDC director Cal Terhune announced, "Repeat offenders are hereby put on notice. If you return to prison, you will face some very serious consequences for your criminal lifestyle."[87]

*   *   *

Cliff has been struck out by "three-strikes," and he knows firsthand what it is to return to the streets destined for failure. "The problems with recidivism partly involve parole. Temptation is too great for a drug addict and most return to the streets (literally) when they need the support of a controlled environment, like a halfway house. It simply makes no sense to work on legislation [to reform the Board of Prison Terms and "Three-Strikes"] and not be prepared to provide individuals with drug programs, counseling, education, vocations and jobs on the streets."

Lewis returned to prison after 1½ years of daily hand-to-mouth struggling to make it, and two drug addiction relapses. He returned defeated, discouraged and reinforced—both from within and by the system—that he is a hopeless loser. Those who see themselves as losers, and who lack hope that things can ever get better, are those most likely to do crime and to be least deterred by the consequences—what have they to lose?

As with so many others in similar circumstances, Lewis had about as much chance of making it on his own, as a pet canary set "free" in a forest. As he sees it, "Maybe it's better this way. At least here I know how to make it."

                    *   *   *

Learning to Cope (C. Lloyd Bailey)
Sometimes freedom is a trap
Life,
When you've been in prison for years and years,
When you have been dehumanized at every
turn,
When you've survived by becoming a robot,
When you've been released with no money,
When you have few or no job skills,
When there is no place as home,
When old friends are gone or must be avoided,
Then freedom is a fantasy,
It's just another trap!

Put All Together

The Little Hoover Commission's (studies California's government and agencies) January 1998 "Report on Corrections in California" soberly and succinctly portrays the system as dysfunctional and failing, and offers both critique and recommendations for a total revamping of both the underlying philosophy and the penal systems themselves:

"After a construction boom of historic proportion, the prisons are now more overcrowded than ever before. Preventing riots and escapes and making room for nearly 10,000 additional inmates each year have become the overriding focus."

"Popular wisdom holds that the way to protect the public from crime is to send criminals to prison. But that idea is undermined by the reality that nine out of ten prisoners are released back into the community."

"The statistics illustrate that locking up criminals is only half the job of protecting public safety. The other half is taking advantage of the time offenders spend in state custody—in prison and on parole—to prepare them to function as responsible citizens, prevent them from committing future crimes and cycling back into prison."

"...the failure of parolees to reintegrate into society exacts another cost: more crimes and more victims, demonstrating that public safety is ill served by a corrections strategy that only protects the public when the inmate is in custody and does not prepare the inmate to be a responsible citizen..."

"In 1977, indeterminate sentencing...was replaced by determinate sentencing. (It) specifically abandoned rehabilitation as a purpose of prison and established punishment as the goal..."

"Because determinate sentencing defines the precise term an offender will serve...inmates and parolees have little incentive to cooperate in programs that might reduce their criminal behavior."[88]

*   *   *

Equating incarceration with justice, and human warehousing with creating a safe society, is morally wrong and an expensive exercise in societal self-deception, and it is failing miserably. Locking away societal problems—drug and alcohol addiction, mental illness, poverty, illiteracy—and using prisons as substitutes for treatment and compassion is a societal crime. And "the People" are being punished along with those imprisoned.

Besides the tremendous financial cost of incarcerating more and more of our neighbors for longer and longer as punishment for lesser and lesser crimes, and seeing the physical consequences in decaying schools, parks and roads, there are other less obvious—but no less terrible—human and societal costs of dehumanizing and debilitating them.

As a society, we are creating many of the monsters we are punishing, and we have set up a brutal cycle of taking people who are redeemable and, like Dr. Frankenstein, forming social misfits. **Few** leave prison better prepared to be a good citizen than when they entered. **All** prisoners learn the values and means of survival in a brutal and depersonalized environment. To some degree, most lose whatever level of social skills, conscience and sense of community responsibility they may have had, as well as self-esteem and confidence. Many will leave with more anger and less respect for law, after having been brutalized by the system and many of its agents which purport to represent "law-abiding civilization."

After spending 38 of his 56 years in prison, recently paroled Dwight E. Abbott, who was a member of a prominent white gang, said about his own experience, "In prison, the only protection you have is your race. All free-world prejudices become obvious and intense inside because of the necessity of survival. Only your own will protect you, and there's safety in numbers." And speaking of parole, "Just deciding to be a good citizen isn't enough. Without assistance, convicts must turn to the same people they turned to in prison. Even trying to put their best foot forward, they're marked as prisoner."[89]

The author of *Changing Lenses* offers a poignant summary of what happens to many men in prison, and why it is that the choice to throw stones often becomes a boomerang, returning to hit "the People" who throw them too indiscriminately, both in their pocketbooks and where they live:

> *"[A prisoner] will learn that conflict is normal, that violence is the great problem solver, that one must be violent to survive, that one responds to frustrations with violence. That is after all, normal in the distorted world of prison…*

> *"This offender got in trouble in part because of a poor sense of self-worth and of personal autonomy, personal power. Yet the prison experience will further strip away his sense of worth and autonomy, leaving him fewer resources for obtaining a sense of worth and autonomy in legitimate ways."*

> *"The entire prison is structured to dehumanize. Prisoners are given numbers, standardized clothing, and little or no personal space. They are denied almost all possibilities for personal decision and power…Our offender got in trouble because of his inability to be self-governing…Prison will further deprive him of that ability."*

One option a prisoner has, in response to his confinement, is rebellion. This, of course, leads to more punishment and deprivation, and sets in place a downhill spiral.

> *"[Another] option is to become devious, to appear to conform while finding ways to retain areas of personal freedom. This leads to another lesson learned in prison, the lesson that manipulation is normal. That is, after all, how one copes in prison. And it is how prison authorities manage prisoners…the convict learns to con…"*

> *"In prison, our offender will absorb a warped ideal of interpersonal relationships. Domination will be the goal…caring will be seen as weakness. And the weak are meant to be preyed upon."*

He will have little encouragement or opportunity to make choices and take responsibility…what he will learn is dependence…" "Some prisoners…commit crimes upon release precisely so they can come back to a place that is familiar…where they have the skills to cope."[90]

Asked to comment on the gruesome, racially motivated hate crime in which black James Byrd, Jr., was dragged to death behind a pickup by John William King (a recently released white parolee) Abbot observed, "Society and its prison instruments made Jasper, Texas. That's prison rage expressing itself. This wasn't the first time, and it won't be the last. Society doesn't want to face it, but as long as we continue to rely on the violent instrument of the modern American prison, we're in for a lot of trouble."[91]

*   *   *

There are some in the system—judges, lawyers, politicians, jailers—who see what I see and feel what I feel. A few of them are courageous enough to try to change the system and to speak the truth, rather than parrot the polls, but most resign themselves—like Pilate—to the political realities that defying the shouts of the crowds for crucifixion—a frenzy they themselves frenetically fan—leads to dead-ended political careers.

Knowing I was working on this book, a lawyer friend sent this unsolicited reflection:

> *"It is so sad to think of the penal process. How it is programmed to dehumanize and destroy whatever potential exists in those it ensnares. Our system goes way beyond antiquity's harsh, simplistic eye for an eye.*

> *"Without pausing to consider the mental, emotional and cultural disabilities of the criminal perpetrators whom we punish, society indiscriminately attempts to extract the 'final solution' from each. Whether annihilated by execution, three strikes and life, or by a knife on the yard on the eve of parole, the social consensus is that justice was done.*

> *"The process is even more insidious with parolees who are dropped from the roof without any means to fly. The crash is virtually inevitable. Annihilation. The few who manage a soft landing are, for the most part, marginalized to a life term of* struggle.

> *"It is frightening to note in these techno-times the lack of social reformers (who are heeded) in comparison with those of the late 19th and early 20th centuries. Care to guess what it will look like 100 years from now?"*

*   *   *

"The degree of civilization in a society can be judged by entering its prisons."

(Fyodor Dostoevsky)

Discussion Guide—Chapter II

1) What is your response to the concept of a "prison-industrial complex" (i.e. politicians, government employees, suppliers, privately owned prison corporations and others who benefit from "tough on crime" rhetoric and laws) as the primary cause of prison overcrowding and expansion?

2) Is your thinking about the purposes and goals of incarceration affected by knowing the prison population is comprised of inmates who are illiterate (up to 70%), drug or alcohol addicted (up to 80%), seriously mentally ill (up to 16%), women who leave behind parentless children?

3) From what you've read so far, has your sense of "good guys" vs "bad guys" changed any? Explain your response.

4) You—as one of "the People"—maintain the prison system. From what you have read, are there any reforms you would support?

5) What personal and practical consequences impact you and your community by California's 75% recidivism rate (about 65% nationally)?

Taken from *Peace and Justice Shall Embrace* by A. Companion.
Published by Writers Club Press an imprint of iUniverse.com.

III—CHOOSE LIFE

On Christmas Day, 1998, Pope John Paul II called for a universal ban on use of the death penalty. That same month, Bulgaria and Lithuania joined the long list of nations which have implemented that ban, leaving the United States as one of the few countries—and the only Western industrialized one—which not only imposes capital punishment, but which continually expands the crimes and lowers the age for its imposition.

A month later, in St. Louis, Missouri, the Pope proclaimed, "A sign of hope is the increasing recognition that the dignity of human life must never be taken away, even in the case of someone who has done great evil. Modern society has the means of protecting itself, without definitively denying criminals the chance to reform. I renew the appeal…to end the death penalty, which is both cruel and unnecessary."[1]

On Good Friday 1999—the Christian memorial day of the execution of an innocent man, the victim of political expediency and mob psychology—the American Catholic bishops reiterated their long standing rejection of the death penalty:

> *"…we join our Holy Father and once again call for the abolition of the death penalty. We urge all people of good will, particularly Catholics, to work to end capital punishment.*

> *"…through prayer and contemplation on the life of Jesus, we must commit ourselves to persistent and principled witness against the death penalty, against a culture of death, and for the Gospel of life."*

*   *   *

"Since the 1976 Supreme Court's reinstatement of the death penalty, [682 prisoners—as of mid-December 2000] have been poisoned, electrocuted, gassed, hanged or faced a firing squad at points across the nation. Texas has claimed a full third of these killings, just over 200 to date."[2] In December 2000, nearly 580 men and women sat on death row in California alone. Over the massive, fortress-like doors which lead into the cavernous and decrepit five-tiered death row at San Quentin State Prison, a sign starkly defines the purpose and contents within—"Condemned."

"Nationally, there were 98 executions in 1999, the largest number since 1954. As of April 1999, 3,652 people were waiting on death rows across the country. In recent years, Congress and the Supreme Court have sought to speed up the pace of executions by limiting the number of appeals inmates can file.[3]

The arguments for and against the death penalty, as with abortion, are well known, and in both issues they tend to become more visceral and emotional than rational. While I will reference some of the arguments against capital punishment—it does not deter crime, it is applied inequitably to minorities and the poor, it is more costly to prosecute and carry out than life in prison, it is not infrequently imposed on the mentally ill and on those (later) determined to have been innocent, it is revenge motivated—my focus will be primarily that of the "Gospel of life" of which the bishops' speak, as contrasted with the "culture of death," and the overall thrust of this book, which is a call to a more noble way, a plea to witness to deeper and more authentic human and Christian capabilities.

I have to hope that even proponents of capital punishment, who sincerely believe that "an eye for an eye" is doing justice, and who find no higher call in the life-example and teachings of Jesus, are nonetheless stirred in some inexplicable way by the witness of those who plead for mercy for—or seek reconciliation with—those who have committed crimes against them. They have something without which the rest of us are incomplete.

*   *   *

When I joined the protestors outside San Quentin prison the day "the People" had set for Robert Harris to die in the gas chamber, and for California to once again join the ranks of the states practicing capital punishment, I was motivated to make a statement against what I knew was wrong. In my study of the arguments, and from my prayerful reflections upon the teachings and example of Jesus, I knew *rationally* that capital punishment served no civic purpose, except to invoke a primitive, vengeful rite of "getting even," and that the only way I could support it on specious religious grounds would be from a state of moral amnesia in which I "forgot" my own unmerited redemption through the mercy of God in Christ.

While I do not doubt the sincerity of Christians who support capital punishment, and not wishing to disparage the genuineness of their faith or devotion, I, nonetheless, remain perplexed by their arguments, which seem to me to be Old Testament-based (as though Jesus never said or did anything relevant to the issue), and at the righteous tenaciousness with which "stoning to death" is promoted as an extension of God's justice.

Those who find Old Testament support—even obligation—to impose death for murder,[4] silently overlook its same harsh requirement of death for those guilty of adultery or blaspheming[5]—not to mention cursing or striking one's parents, or working on the Sabbath[6]—among other offenses. If we are going to invoke Old Testament justice, we need to do it across the board and start executing the teenagers who swear at their parents—and their parents for mowing the lawn on the Sabbath, or having an affair at the office. Moses makes no distinctions. Who are we to do otherwise? All these offenses are equally "mortal" (capital) sins. Invoking Old Testament justice will leave few of us to implement it.

But, apart from the letter of the law, religious people are challenged to live out of, and to promote, the *spirit* of the law. Behind even the most harsh Old Testament mandates is God's ultimate purpose—the claiming and redeeming of a people to be his own. Restoration—not destruction, life—not death, is what God wills.

Once I began living among convicted murderers and others convicted of violent and serious crimes, and now that some of my closest friends include them, I've come to *know* other truths which are not easily reduced to the simplistic, rational categories of guilty/innocent, true/false, right/wrong, sinful/moral. The complexity of human beings—thoughts, actions, culpability—and the array of factors forming the persons we become—family, neighborhood, genes, diet, education, mental condition, life experiences and deprivations—make it impossible to reduce much that is human to a black or white judgment, and absurd to identify any human person by any one act or aspect of his/her intricate reality.

I know too many people who committed murder who are not murderers, whose crime was an isolated moment in an otherwise nonviolent lifestyle, and who pose absolutely no more danger to society than those who sat on their juries. I've listened to too many life-stories to believe justice can be done by taking life, rather than nurturing life. I know too many men who are no longer the person who committed the crime, who have undergone such a genuine personal and spiritual conversion that it is no stretch of the truth to say they are strangers to their former selves. And I know scandalously far too many men who would not be here at all if they weren't black, illiterate, mentally ill or too poor to have had adequate legal assistance. Neither incarceration in general, nor the death penalty in particular, are acted out on a level playing field, or imposed justly. This *alone* should be enough to make "the People" queasy about standing in capital judgment of anyone.

*   *   *

"Perhaps the bleakest fact of all is that the death penalty is imposed not only in a freakish and discriminatory manner, but also in some cases upon defendants who are actually innocent."[7]

(U.S. Supreme Court Justice William J. Brennan, 1994)

*   *   *

The Chicago Tribune examined all 285 death penalty convictions in Illinois since capital punishment was restored in 1977. It concluded that the cases were "riddled with faulty evidence, incompetent lawyers and unscrupulous trial tactics." To win cases, prosecutors repeatedly exaggerated criminal backgrounds of defendants, and sometimes withheld information which would have called their guilt into question.

Appeals are in process in 259 of the cases. New trials or sentences have been ordered in 127 cases. [Thirteen] people, who were condemned to death, have been completely exonerated, and another 74 have had their sentences reduced to something less than death. In at least 33 cases, the attorneys who represented those sentenced to death were later disbarred or suspended.[8]

In three cases, students working on class projects at Northwestern University were able to find evidence that had escaped defense lawyers. While a proper defense of a death penalty case costs $250,000 and takes months of research, defendants in these cases were often represented by lawyers paid a few thousand dollars—or less—and who spent only two days in preparation.

On January 31, 2000, Illinois Gov. George Ryan announced a moratorium on executions, and has appointed a commission to study what went wrong and why. "I now favor a moratorium because I have grave concerns about our state's shameful record of convicting innocent people and putting them on death row."[9] And this is just *one* state!

Nationwide, 85 death row inmates have been found innocent since 1973. In 1997, the American Bar Association called for a national moratorium. "We are learning that a lot of mistakes are made, and errors cannot easily be rectified after someone's execution," said Jerome Shestack, former ABA president. Legislatures in 16 (of the 38 states with the death penalty) are now considering abolishing the death penalty, imposing a moratorium or reviewing death penalty laws. California is not among them.[10]

*   *   *

The most far reaching study of the death penalty in the U.S. found that two out of three convictions were overturned on appeal. The study, released in June 2000, was conducted by a team of lawyers and criminologists at Columbia University on all aspects of capital sentences from 1973 to 1995. It found a national average appeals rate of 68%. California's rate was 87%. Three states had a 100% overturn rate (Kentucky, Maryland, Tennessee), while Virginia had 18%, by far the lowest. The conviction reversals were due to: incompetent defense (37%); misconduct by police or prosecutors in suppressing evidence that would have helped the defendant (19%); bias on the part of a judge or jury (5%); faulty jury instructions (20%). The remaining 19% were in a miscellaneous category that included coerced confessions and keeping black persons off the jury when a black person was on trial.[11]

*   *   *

> *"I have often heard people who never participated in an execution say they would be more than willing to pull the switch, drop the pellet, or inject the needle. On the other hand, I have never heard anyone who has participated in an execution say, 'I would like to do that again.'*

> *"I have found that the person we execute is not necessarily the same person he was when the crime was committed years earlier.*

In one case that still troubles me, an inmate had been on death row for seven or eight years. During that time he underwent a significant change in his life. His was not a last-minute acknowledgment of Christian redemption, but one that occurred several years previously. While strapped to the electric chair, just moments before the death penalty was carried out, the inmate asked permission to pray. He prayed for his own forgiveness, for those who were about to execute him, and for his victim's family.

"I believe individuals have the ability to change. In the time a person spends on death row, some rather dramatic changes can occur. I always will wonder about the good this man might have accomplished if his sentence had been commuted to life without parole."[12]

(Morris L. Thigpen, former commissioner, Alabama Dept. of Corrections)

*   *   *

While some states have well-funded capital defender offices, Alabama, with the fastest growing death row in the nation, has none. Court-appointed attorneys are paid so little, many lawyers refuse to take the cases. So, often, young, inexperienced lawyers, or those who make their living from court appointments, take the work. Mike Williams had never even read the entire death penalty statute before he was appointed to represent a man in 1987 (who died of cancer on death row). He ended up making $4.98 an hour "to prepare for the defense of a human's life."[13]

California has a shortage of lawyers willing to take capital cases, mainly because they usually lose money on them and don't want the aggravation of a case that means life or death. In 1998, the Legislature increased attorney's rates to a maximum $125 an hour—about one-third what corporate attorneys receive—plus expenses. That still doesn't cover costs. In 1997, the Legislature established the Habeas Corpus Resource Center, which is a state-run law firm to represent condemned inmates, but the backlog of unrepresented inmates continues.[14]

*   *   *

In response to the Texas execution of born-again Christina Karla Faye Tucker, Rev. Pat Robertson, head of the Christian Coalition and formerly a strong supporter of the death penalty, called for a vast public relations campaign to undercut public support for the death penalty. Echoing the Pope's references to a "culture of death," Robertson said, "We need to be pro-life across the board."

Of Tucker, Rev. Robertson exclaimed, "The woman who had been convicted wasn't there any longer. This was a different person. To execute her was an act of barbarism which was totally unnecessary." Of the celebrating crowd outside the prison, he questioned, "What kind of animal vengeance is it in a society where people take such delight in this?"[15]

*   *   *

"I've known more than 200 convicted murders...I've prayed with these people and listened as they've expressed their feelings—guilt and remorse, frustration and anger. I've heard their life stories, including stories of conversion and faith. This is what prison ministry is all about."

"People sometimes tell me that a person who has committed murder has lost not only his civil rights, but his rights as a child of God and no longer deserves to be treated with respect. When did God say that? Have people who think that way received a special revelation?

"I do not minimize the evil of murder and the harm it does. Murder, like all crime, has a ripple effect. The pain experienced by the victim's family and friends lasts for years, sometimes for the whole of life."

"Opposing the death penalty does not mean siding with the offender against the victim—it means recognizing that each person is a child of God...I suppose it's my advantage as a prison chaplain that all the murderers I know have names, faces and personalities, and most have the desire to find and accept Jesus Christ."

"Most of the murderers I've met are filled with the pain of guilt for what they did, pain for the pain they caused the victim's families and their own families. Some people say, 'Good! That's how it should be.' But I am there to encourage their conversion, and that can only come about by treating them with respect. Not excusing, not justifying, but making them aware that they, too, can receive God's forgiveness."

"Some people say that everyone who deliberately kills someone should be executed. There are about 30,000 murders a year in the United States. Do we really want 20,000 executions yearly—55 a day, seven days a week? The number of inmates on Death Row is now about 3,500. They are overwhelmingly poor and Black or Latino. The death penalty reflects, I believe, the attitude of a 'disposable society' toward certain of its members.

"This is an attitude shared even by ourselves as members of the Church. We tend to avoid the really tough work. We evangelize—up to a point. We forgive—up to a point. We respect—up to a point. But we do not forgive or respect certain people, so we neither evangelize them nor want them to be evangelized."

"Not all murderers will experience religious conversion. Nor will all repent and seek forgiveness. But whether they do or don't, all are children of God."[16]

(Deacon George W. Brooks)

*   *   *

Despite a series of court orders reversing restrictions imposed by San Quentin authorities upon the right of condemned inmates to receive spiritual support, oppressive restrictions continue, including: requiring the spiritual advisor to leave 45 minutes prior to execution (leaving the inmate alone and without support in his final moments before death); requiring ministers to be strip searched prior to visiting (and after leaving to use the restroom).

It took court orders to allow condemned inmates to receive Communion before their executions, for ministers to touch them or hold their hands, and for the ministers to receive a drink of water.[17]

*   *   *

"If Manuel Babbitt, a former Vietnam veteran, tortured by postwar mental disorders, had been kept safely in a mental hospital, if he had gotten the help he needed, he [and his victim] would not have died the way they did,"said his brother Bill, after the execution at San Quentin on May 5, 1999.[18]

In the hours prior to his execution, Babbitt seemed more concerned about others than his pending fate. When told he could spend up to $50 for his last meal, he chose to fast, and asked that the money be given to feed the homeless. When asked by his sister-in-law what she could do for him, he gave her the name of another man on death row who had no visitors and asked her to visit him. In his last visits with his family, he asked them not to be bitter.

"Some hate Mannie so much they don't want to see that human face. They want the face of a monster," said Bill the day before his brother's death. "Hate is going to be the rule of the day. And by the time they figure out how wrong this is, sometime down the line in history, it's going to be too late for the Babbitt family.

"…Governor Davis is worried about victims? Well, what about us? We're victims, too."

Linda observed, "It's not going to help. Hate doesn't die. It just lives on. It will find somewhere else to live and breathe. It won't ease their [the victim's family] pains."[19]

*   *   *

African Americans are disproportionately sentenced to die for committing capital crimes because of rampant racism in the nation's criminal justice system, according to a May 1999 report, "Killing With Prejudice: Race and the Death Penalty," prepared by Amnesty International USA. The report is consistent with numerous other studies.

The report documents racial bias of every step of the judicial process—from police to prosecutors to judges to jurors. Of 500 prisoners executed between 1977 and 1998, 81.8% were convicted of killing a white person, even though African Americans and whites are homicide victims in almost equal numbers nationwide. African Americans who kill whites are 11 times more likely to receive the death penalty than whites who kill African Americans.[20]

A U.S. Justice Department study released September 12, 2000, found wide racial and geographic disparities in the federal death penalty system. Attorney General Janet Reno commented: "At this point we are troubled by the figures, but we have not found the bias. Minorities are over-represented in the federal death penalty system, as both victims and defendants, relative to the general population. Crime is often the product of social ills and harsh conditions such as poverty, drug abuse and lack of opportunity, that disproportionately affect minorities. So long as those conditions remain, we will continue to see disparities in the number of minorities in the criminal justice system."[21]

*   *   *

In 1972 the U.S. Supreme Court ruled the death penalty unconstitutional (as practiced) as "cruel and unusual punishment." Twelve states continue to ban the imposition of the death penalty, while others, such as California, have refined both its laws and procedures of implementation to meet the court's objections. In 1978, California voters reinstated the death penalty through a state proposition, and expanded the categories for which it can be applied in March 2000.

What is accepted as "normal" in the United States is considered barbaric just about everywhere else. A total of 105 countries have abandoned the death penalty, either by law or defacto. In 1998, 68 people were executed in the U.S., behind only China (1,067) and Congo (100).[22]

The U.S. Supreme Court has ruled that there are no constitutional barriers to executing people who are mentally retarded, or juveniles. The court has also said "if they were to respond to the racial discrimination apparent in death penalty cases, lawyers soon would be raising the issue of racial disparity in sentencing in other cases [for lesser offenses]." "The Court said that certain disparities based on race in the administration of criminal punishment are *inevitable*." Justice William Brennan accused his colleagues of having a "fear of too much justice."[23]

Support for the death penalty in California has gradually declined from a high of 83% in 1996 to slightly over 70% in 1999, with about the same number of people favoring speeding up the process and restricting appeals.[24] A June 2000 Field Poll showed a decline to 63% of California adults supporting capital punishment, whereas 73% supported a moratorium for study of the fairness with which the death penalty is applied. A Gallup Poll of about the same time showed national support for the death penalty had dropped to 66%.[25]

*   *   *

In 1996, Congress passed the U.S. Anti-Terrorism and Effective Death Penalty Act. The intent of the law is to shorten the time between imposition of a death sentence and its execution. Once a condemned person has exhausted appeals on the state level, Federal court trial judges have a year to rule on a case, and appellate judges only four months.

"…Congress said a state could qualify for the fast-track provisions only if it had a firmly established mechanism for appointing, paying and funding for expenses of competent death penalty defense lawyers. **No state has qualified so far.**"

Since 1998, only 38 of the 563 men and women on California's death row have had lawyers appointed to handle their appeals. These could qualify for the fast-track provisions when they reach the federal courts. Lawyers are being appointed now for those sentenced in 1995 and 1996.

About 160 inmates have no legal representation for their first appeals to the California Supreme Court, another 45 have no assistance with the habeas corpus appeals. Historically, the U.S. Supreme Court had voided about 40% of death sentences because of violations of the U.S. Constitution.[26]

*   *   *

Journalists are suing to allow the public the "right" to view the entire process of preparing to execute a condemned person. Presently, the inmate is strapped to the table, with the IV tubes inserted and ready to receive the poisons, before the viewing window is opened.

The journalists proposed using surgical masks to protect the identity of the execution team. Prison officials expressed concern the inmates might tear off the masks, and objected to creating "the appearance of a surgical procedure." The journalists countered with the suggestion of using riot helmets with face shields. San Quentin's acting warden responded that would interfere with "bonding with the inmate. That bond is very important to the process of carrying out the execution in a professional, very humane way."[27]

*   *   *

A New York Times national study, released in September 2000, showed that the 12 states without the death penalty have not had higher homicide rates than those that do. In fact,

10 of the 12 have rates lower than the national average. Over the 20 years of the study, states with the death penalty have had 48% to 101% higher homicide rates than the states without it. "It is difficult to make a case for any deterrent effect from these numbers," said criminologist Steven Messner of State University of New York at Albany.[28]

*   *   *

Roman Catholic tradition has always resisted the death penalty, even while allowing it when it was the only means to protect society in the eras prior to the development of our modern prison systems, which provide secure confinement for those who pose a real danger to society.

"St. Augustine taught that the death penalty should never be used, even for those who have committed the most horrible crimes. He taught that the dignity of the sinner remains the same as the dignity of the saint."

"St. Thomas [Aquinas] likewise argued that if a condemned criminal could be incarcerated, then society and the common good would be protected, and justification for the death penalty would be nullified."

In his 1995 letter, "The Gospel of Life," Pope John Paul II all but excluded moral justification for implementation of the death penalty, "today…as a result of steady improvements in the organization of the penal system [justification is] very rare, if not practically non-existent." (#56).

The *Catechism of the Catholic Church* says, "Today…the cases in which the execution of the offender is an absolute necessity are 'very rare, if not practically non-existent.'"(#2267)[29]

*   *   *

In their 1999 pastoral letter, "The Gospel of Life and Capital Punishment," the California Catholic Conference of Bishops called upon "faithful Catholics and all people of good will to reflect on respect for all human life, even life perceived as guilty, expendable, and perhaps even morally repulsive," saying they "have the responsibility to call all Americans to conversion, including political leaders, and especially those publicly identified as Catholic."

> *"It is our firm conviction that we must never as individuals or as a society suspend the principle of the right to life. By abolishing the death penalty, we would make a powerful statement in favor of life and reaffirm our belief that God grants all people the opportunity for conversion, reconciliation and reparation for evil done."*

> *"…Catholics do not accept abortion as a solution to unwanted or unintended pregnancy, nor euthanasia or assisted suicide as a solution to*

unrelenting physical pain. In like manner, Catholics should not accept capital punishment as a solution to the problem of violence and murder.[30]

In 1999, religious leaders representing Christian, Jewish, Muslim and Buddhist traditions, coming together as *California People of Faith Working Against the Death Penalty*, issued a "Statement of Conscience":

"We are deeply disturbed by violent crime and are grieved by the suffering of its victims... We affirm that the people in our communities are entitled to protection from those who would do harm.

"We acknowledge that violent actions have consequences, that offenders should be held accountable, and that communities need ways to find healing.

We affirm that restitution to victims and their loved ones, and rehabilitation of the offender should be our goals rather than punishment meted out for its own sake or in a spirit of vengeance.

"In that spirit we affirm the strong teachings of our respective faith communities which hold that capital punishment is not an appropriate response to these problems. We believe that the death penalty is morally untenable, particularly when we have the means necessary to protect ourselves from those who would kill. Violence is simply not the answer to the problem of violence.

"...California now has the largest death row in the United States and continues to expand the categories of capital crimes at an alarming rate. Legislation is currently proposed which would truncate the appeals process and lead to a significant increase in the number of executions...which would, by necessity, include the mentally retarded and those with other mental dysfunction, children, those poorly represented in court, and the innocent."

"...We invite all people of good will to join us in choosing moral courage over fear and creative solutions over ineffective responses to questions of violent crime and punishment."[31]

*   *   *

When Christians don't find anything incongruous about yelling, "Crucify him!," in response to the sins of another, and, when Christians give up on the power of God to work for conversion and redemption in any human heart, then the good news of the Good News has become "salt which has lost its flavor."

When, as "the People," we condemn someone to death, we are saying, "You have no value. Your life has no meaning to us. You are beyond hope of redemption." Those are words which should cause a Christian to choke.

> *"A man came up to me after my father was murdered and said, 'I hope they fry those people. I hope they fry them so you and your family can get some peace.' I know that man meant to comfort me, but it was the most horrible thing he could possibly have said. Before my father's murder I had evolved a set of values that included a respect for life and an opposition to the death penalty. For me to change my beliefs because my father was murdered would only give more power to his killers, for they would then take not only his life but his main legacy to me: the values he instilled. The same is true for society. If we let murderers turn us to murder, we give them too much power. They succeed in bringing us to their way of thinking and acting, and we become what we say we abhor."*
>
> (Renny Cushing, Hampton, New Hampshire)[32]

When we judiciously kill to demonstrate how abhorrent killing is, we diminish for a second time the sacredness of every human life.

Discussion Guide—Chapter III

a) Which, if any, of the major arguments against capital punishment are persuasive to you?
    1. It does not deter crime.
    2. It is applied inequitably to minorities and the poor.
    3. It is more costly than life in prison.
    4. It is imposed on the mentally ill and innocent.
    5. It is revenge motivated.
    6. It is morally wrong.

b) How does knowing that over 3,500 men and women in this country are awaiting execution affect your feelings about capital punishment?

c) If one of the persons condemned to death were your parent, child or close friend—someone you knew, instead of a statistic—how would that affect your feelings about capital punishment?

d) What is the author trying to say when he contends that "not every person who commits murder is a murderer?"

e) Should a death sentence be mitigated in some way for persons who show genuine remorse, repentance and conversion of heart?

f) Since our modern prison system and sentences of life without possibility of parole provide full protection to society from those who pose a danger to it, are you ready to join Pope John Paul II's plea to end the death penalty? Give your reasons.

IV—THE CORNERSTONE

There is a story told of two Irish clans whose feud had gone on for so many generations no one any longer knew what had begun the animosity eons ago, but it was so intense God could no longer handle it. One day he decided to intervene by confronting the leader of the larger clan as he plowed his field one day.

"Seamus! This is God speaking. I've watched for generations with great sadness as your clan and Sean's have fought and vilified each other. It is time to break the vicious cycle. I have a proposition for you, which I hope will help you understand I love all my children, and that it is my intention that you reconcile and live as brothers and sisters. I am going to grant you any one wish you want for yourself."

"Me, Lord? Any wish I want? Does that mean you are taking my side against Sean and his dirty…" "Stop! There is one condition to my offer. Whatever you ask for yourself, Sean will get twice." "What! What! Do you mean, if I ask to live 500 years, Sean will live 1000?" "Yes!" "And, if I ask for a million dollars, Sean will get two million?" "Yes, that is exactly what I mean. I want you to learn to love your neighbor as yourself."

After a few minutes of silent pondering, Seamus responds, "Well, Lord, you drive a hard bargain, but it will be worth it. I'll take *one* glass eye!"

*   *   *

Jesus was a great storyteller. His parables, metaphors and similes remain an important part of our vocabulary and culture two thousand years later. Whether one believes him to be the incarnate Word of God, or only a great prophet, the clarity and simplicity of his teachings, and their powerful, attracting—yet challenging—insights into both human and divine nature, permeate personal religious faith and our communal values as a nation.

For Christians, of course, Jesus *is* the Word of God, who has come as light to dispel darkness, and whose words are those of the Father who sent him.[1] Underlying both the mission and message of Jesus is that he has come as reconciler and healer. The teachings and stories of Jesus begin with the call to change one's way of thinking, valuing and living, and to allow God's mercy and love to become the fount out of which one draws new and eternal life.[2]

Jesus has come to reestablish peace—shalom—between God and God's people. His life, death and resurrection show us the way to the "peace which surpasses understanding," which we do not merit by being worthy or sinless, which we cannot earn by being "good," and which we can only accept as a freely given gift of love—grace. God reconciles us to himself in Jesus. Compassion and mercy are God's ways of doing justice. Our sins merit retribution, but we find ourselves restored in grace instead. The Scriptures hold incredible hope for the redemption of every person.

The Old Testament covenant was established by God to give the Hebrews ways and an understanding of how to work toward shalom—how to be right with God and one's neighbors. Hebrew ideas of law and justice were radically different from Hammurabi's because of covenant and shalom. God was the source of all authority and law, not the king, and God was personal, faithful and concerned about his people, especially the poor and downtrodden.[3]

The Ten Commandments and the Torah (as with the New Covenant established by Jesus, and in the Sermon on the Mount) were not abstract laws to follow, but an invitation and a promise: "If you keep the commandments and live by the Covenant, this is what you will be like and how life will be in your community." The Law was for redemption and life. Overtime this was forgotten, and laws multiplied and became rigidly codified. Soon the law became more important than the spirit out of which it was given, and than the relationships between God and his people, and the people among themselves. It is this that Jesus rejected when he insisted that the law was to serve the good of people, not the other way around.[4]

Some historians hold that biblical concepts of justice were later mixed with Greco-Roman. In the confluence, the purposes of retribution and punishment lost their rootedness as components of reestablishing shalom, and became ends in themselves. This new hybrid then *appeared* to have biblical foundations, leading later generations (including our own) to interpret the Bible through distorted lenses.[5]

Restitution, vindication of injuries inflicted and wrongs done, and reconciliation were components of restoring shalom—of making things right between the persons involved, and with God and the community. Offenders need to be held accountable: to understand and acknowledge the harm done, and to take steps to make things right. Biblically, confession, repentance, punishment and restitution are intimately interwoven; *together* they seek restoration of *all* involved. Punishment was not an end in itself; it was not to break and destroy the offender. Limits were set upon punishments which could be inflicted and they had to be proportionate to the offenses.

Biblically, society's self-interest, as well as the needs of the offender, dictates that doing justice include seeking the good and restoration of the offender. God's justice is done not because it is deserved, but because it is needed.[6]

*   *   *

We are so conditioned from infancy that we are loved and have value because we "do good"—make mother smile, get "A's" on our report cards, win the trophy, become "successful," go to church—that either our illusion of righteousness, or our delusion of hopeless sinfulness, lead us to deny grace. Deep inside us, we wrestle with the notion of "cheap grace" which we haven't earned, and which God can lavish as generously on my clan or yours, on the "good" and the "bad" without preference or discrimination. When we demand that "justice be done," we are not celebrating grace, but asking for glass eyes.

Nonetheless, the words and modeling of God-in-Jesus are constantly those of grace-is-justice, reconciliation-is-peace, mercy and compassion-are-love:

> *"I say to you, love your enemies, and pray for those who persecute you, that you may be children of your heavenly Father, for he makes his sun rise on the bad and the good, and causes his rain to fall on the just and unjust."*[7]

> *"Blessed are the merciful, for they shall be shown mercy."* [8]

> *"God proves his love for us in that while we were still sinners Christ died for us."* [9]

When asked the most important law, Jesus goes to the fundamental core of his religious and moral teaching. He responds that there is only one law—love—and that it has two intertwined and inseparable aspects—love of God with one's whole being, and, *in that love*, love of neighbor as one's self.[10] Jesus goes on to say that he is the model for love of neighbor, and that the love we have received as free gift from God is to be given to others just as freely—and what we hold back, will be held back from us:

> *"This is my commandment: Love one another as I have loved you."* [11]

> *"Why do you notice the splinter in your brother's eye, but do not perceive the wooden beam in your own eye?...the measure with which you measure will be measured out to you."* [12]

Peter asks, "Lord, if my brother sins against me, how often must I forgive him? As many as seven times?" Jesus answered, "I say to you, not seven times but seventy-seven times." Jesus goes on to tell the parable of the unforgiving servant, who, after having been forgiven a huge debt by his master, who had compassion on him, has a fellow servant thrown in prison for a small loan which he cannot repay. Upon learning that his servant has refused mercy as he had received it, the master turns him over "to the torturers until he should pay back the whole debt." Jesus concludes, "So will my heavenly Father do to you, unless each forgives his brother from his heart."[13]

> *"...the one who loves has fulfilled the law. The commandments...are summed up in this saying, 'You shall love your neighbor as yourself.' Love does no evil to the neighbor, hence, love is the fulfillment of the law."* [14]

"We love because he first loved us. If anyone says, 'I love God' but hates his brother, he is a liar; for whoever does not love a brother whom he has seen cannot love God whom he has not seen. This is the commandment we have from him: whoever loves God must also love his brother."[15]

The Our Father prayer is so well known, we easily recite the words without reflecting upon what we are asking God. Do we really want God to "Forgive us our debts *as* we forgive our debtors?" Over and over, Jesus and the New Testament writers remind us that we have been forgiven an unpayable debt, and we are now indebted—by the blood of Christ—to lavish the same unmerited, generous compassion and mercy on our neighbors—no exceptions are given, no exceptions are acceptable.

There is a common assumption that we must punish before we can forgive. In practice, we administer punishment in such a way that it damages the offender and shalom even more, often feels undeserved, and, most often, denies any opportunity for forgiveness.

For healing to take place in both victim and offender, *both* repentance and forgiveness are necessary. Forgiveness does not mean forgetting, nor is it redefining the offenses as a non-offense. Forgiveness is letting go of the power the offense and offender have over the victim, and allowing both the possibility of healing and redemption.[16]

*   *   *

"And who is my neighbor?," begins the most widely known of Jesus' parables. One that captures our imaginations and hearts, because its truth is so compelling and we know, "This is how the world ought to be. This is how I want to be." In the Parable of the Good Samaritan, Jesus chooses as his hero a representative of every despised, rejected and hated person, and touches the raw nerve of every prejudice, pretended superiority, condescending judgment and arms length "other than me" definition we have ever thought, spoke or acted toward another human being, race, ethnic or other group of persons.

In the parable, we see the hypocrisy of our "goodness," the sinfulness or our standoffishness from those who are "they" to us, and we know instinctively how wrong we are about how we love and do justice. After telling the story, Jesus asks, "And who was the neighbor?" The response, "The one who showed mercy." The directive, "Go and do likewise."[17]

As Saul and his posse head for Damascus to arrest the followers of Jesus, he is confronted by the risen Jesus in a dramatic, life-altering encounter. "Saul, Saul, why are you persecuting me?" Who are you, sir?" "I am Jesus, whom you are persecuting."[18]

Saul (soon to be Paul, to indicate his change of heart and life) understands that Jesus is identifying himself with those being persecuted. This indelible lesson becomes Paul's beautiful images of the church as the "body of Christ" in which each member has responsibility for all the others, and, in which, the joy or suffering of any member is felt and shared by all the others. Of all the spiritual gifts with which God has endowed his people, the most important and indispensable one is love. Without love, every other human endeavor is reduced to "resounding gongs and clashing cymbals."[19]

Jesus does not condone crime, but neither does he allow the criminal to be put outside his embrace, he even identifies himself with those in prison and makes clear, "What you do to them, you do to me[20]." When confronting law breakers and sinners, Jesus' primary goal is restoration to grace, restoration to their full potential as children of God—made in God's image—and as brothers/sisters within the community. Jesus' primary goal is shalom, the establishment of peace with God, within the offender, with the community.

Fraudulent tax collectors, who grew rich by preying on their neighbors, heard, "I will stay with you," and, "I have come to seek and to save what was lost."[21] One, Matthew, is chosen to be an apostle. To the church goers who complain, Jesus says, "Go and learn the meaning of the saying, 'I desire mercy, not sacrifice.'"[22]

Jesus' scathing rebuke of the hypocrisy of the religious leaders is a plea to let God cure their blindness so they can see with compassion and act with justice.[23]

The thief crucified with Jesus, who is all too aware of his crimes and guilt, hears the promise, "Today you will be with me in paradise." The soldiers who have mocked, beaten and nailed him to the cross, hear him praying for them, "Father, forgive them!"[24]

The woman caught in adultery is told both, "I do not condemn you," and "Sin no more."[25]

"What if Jesus had…agreed with (the accusers of the adulterous woman) or been a strict interpreter of the law of the time? What if they had stoned her to death, in keeping with the law? What would the effect of that have been on the moral life and development of the people of that village?"

"The question is: Which of these, law or love, must give way when they are in conflict?" "When this whole thing shifts down, if it doesn't leave us more loving and caring, it will leave us worse off as a nation."[26]

Our system of justice focuses on guilt and the past. Biblical justice seeks to solve problems and to make things right for the future. Biblical justice responds because shalom is lacking, and to restore the covenant bonds which are broken. It asks: "Does the outcome work to make things right? Are things being made right for the poor, the least powerful, the lease 'deserving'?"

In biblical justice, people and relationships—not laws, the state or the moral order—are the victims. Biblical justice does not allow the separation of questions about crime from those about poverty and power.[27]

*   *   *

Every community has both the right and responsibility to protect and promote peace and safety, and just laws and just legal systems promote peace *through* justice. Peace is the goal, justice is the means. The teaching of Jesus—repeatedly modeled by him—is that law is just when it promotes peace and does justice with compassion, that law is to serve persons—victims, community and offenders—in a way which restores them. Laws and legal systems which destroy persons, and which lack mercy and compassion are peace destroyers, they fracture the community into clans of "Us" vs "Them," they create a false peace of oppressive and punitive order, under which anger and desire to hurt back fester. Jesus teaches us that the law was made for the good of persons, and when the demands of the law harm, rather than restore persons, neither justice nor shalom have been served.[28]

What do rightfully raging and grieving families of murdered loved ones do, when the murderer's execution they were depending upon fails to ease the pain or bring peace? The attempt to give "two glass eyes" always causes at least one in the person who holds onto hurt or desire for vengeance. Unreconciled anger—no matter how justified in its cause—is like a boomerang thrown—it comes back to the hurler to "take out another eye."

Hurts keep hurting—whether they are the victim's, the offender's or the community's—until they are made redemptive—until they can be redeemed—exchanged for healing—and, if possible, reconciliation. This is at the heart of Christian faith and hope in cross-power, in the efficacy of letting go, of dying to bring forth new life, new possibilities. It is also the base from which love becomes commandment. Just as the seed which refuses to fall to the ground and die will never become life-giving wheat, which is its hidden potential,[29] neither will any human person—especially a Christian—experience the true and full meaning of his/her potential to be redeemed without letting go of the desire to hurt back.

A Christian understanding of peace and justice are countercultural. Turning the other cheek[30] does not come naturally, nor is it easily practiced. We need to be angry when injustices are done and peace is shattered by the criminal acts of our neighbors. A better measure of how deeply the Gospel has permeated our sense of justice and peace, though, is to measure whether or not we get angry with unjust justice systems, or whether we disown the criminal as no longer neighbor or brother/sister. "Be angry but do not sin" by acting unjustly in the name of justice.[31]

When asked if the Reign of God had begun, Jesus gave "the blind see" as the first sign that it had, and when he castigated the Pharisees for using the law to hurt rather than restore their neighbors, he indicted them as "blind" to true fidelity to the law.[32]

Shalom begins in the heart of individuals who have come to understand that *they* are the lost coin, the prodigal son, the wandering lamb which have been sought out and redeemed by Christ, who, as the Divine Physician, came to heal and restore.[33] On the cross, Jesus answers the question, "Is there a possibility that every human being is more than just the worst act of their lives, and that they can be open to redemption?"[34] Each of us who claim Christ as our Lord and Redeemer are acknowledging our own sins, and our dependence upon the mercy and compassion of God. None of us has ever prayed, "Lord, give me what I deserve!" We pray instead, "Lord, have mercy!" "You were ransomed…with the precious blood of Christ…"[35]

While the "peace which surpasses understanding" begins in individual hearts, it is meant to overflow into thanksgiving which is manifested in worship (love of God), and in charity and justice (love of neighbor). What we have been given, we are to multiply and share.[36] If we know the peace of Christ in our hearts, then we are commissioned to be peacemakers. If we claim for ourselves not the punishment we deserve, but God's compassionate justice, then restorative justice is demanded of us. "I have given you a model to follow, so that as I have done for you, you should also do…blessed are you if you do it."[37]

"Justice is not an 'elective' we can choose to ignore. Justice has to do with shalom relationships and thus is fundamental to what God is about, to what God is, and to what we are to be. In fact, justice serves as a measuring stick to test for shalom!

"When the prophets condemned Israel for straying from God, they made it clear that injustice was the problem as much as failure to worship as they ought." The norm for justice arises from God's relationship with Israel. The way God responds to wrongdoing provides an important window into the goals of God's justice.[38]

All this does not mean that those who break the law and harm the peace of the community should not be held accountable, nor does it mean there should not be punishment of prison. It does mean, however, that we refuse to equate punishment with justice, and justice with prison. We commit ourselves—precisely because we are Christians—to practicing justice with the goal of restoring persons to shalom—victims, offenders, community.

Precisely because we are disciples of Jesus, we are committed to doing justice in such a way in which prosecutor, jury members, victims, judge, offenders, legislators, jailers, voters never lose sight of the deepest truth at work—we are all children of God, we are all brothers and sisters, we are all members of the same body, there is only *one* clan.

We are capable of doing restorative justice as long as we remember who we are, and at what cost we have been redeemed. We are capable of rejecting vengeance if we don't forget the "debts" others can claim before God regarding our failings. "If you, Lord, mark our sins, Lord, who can stand?"[39] We are capable of redesigning just justice systems, if we keep our eyes on the modeling of Jesus, and, if we listen for the words of God's Spirit in the confused debates about crime and proper responses, we might hear:

> "…Do not repay anyone evil for evil; be concerned for what is noble…If possible, on your part, live at peace with all…do not look for revenge…rather, if

your enemy is hungry, feed him…Do not be conquered by evil, but conquer evil with good."[40]

*   *   *

"The vengeful will suffer the Lord's vengeance,
for he remembers their sins in detail.
Forgive your neighbor's injustice;
then when you pray, your sins will be forgiven.
Could anyone nourish anger against another,
and expect healing from the Lord?
Could anyone refuse mercy to another,
yet seek pardon for his own sins?
If he who is but flesh cherishes wrath,
who will forgive his sins?"
(Sirach 28:1–5)

Concepts of Justice—Biblical and Modern[41]

Contemporary Justice	Biblical Justice
1. Justice separated into areas, each with different rules.	1. Justice seen as an integrated whole.
2. Justice is an inquiry into guilt.	2. Justice is a search for solutions.
3. Justice tested by rules and proper procedures.	3. Justice defined by outcome, substance.
4. Focus on punishment.	4. Focus on making things right.
5. Punishment is an end in itself.	5. Punishment is within context of seeking redemption and shalom.
6. Rewards based on just deserts, "deserved."	6. Justice based on need, undeserved.
7. Justice opposed to mercy.	7. Justice based on mercy and love.
8. Justice neutral, claiming to treat all equally.	8. Justice both fair and partial, taking into account personal needs.
9. Justice as maintenance of the status quo	9. Justice as active, progressive, seeking to transform status quo.
10. Focus on guilt and abstract principles.	10. Focus on harm done.
11. Wrong of violation of rules.	11. Wrong as violation of people, relationships, shalom.
12. Guilt is unforgivable.	12. Guilt is forgivable (although an obligation remains).
13. Differentiates between "offenders" and others.	13. Recognizes we are all offenders, family.
14. Individual solely responsible.	14. Individual responsible, but seen within social and political contexts.
15. Focus on letter of law	15. Spirit of law most important.
16. State is victim.	16. People, shalom are victims.
17. Justice tends to divide people.	17. Justice aims to bring people together.

Discussion Guide—Chapter IV

1) How would you explain to your child the irrational—and often brutal—clan conflicts they witness in places like Kosovo or Northern Ireland, or the racial and anti-Semitic hate crimes that plague our own nation?

2) The author uses the image of Jesus as modeling "grace-is-justice, reconciliation-is-peace, mercy and compassion-are-love." How could you use this image in your own life and relationships?

3) Since we are all sinners, how can any of us stand in judgment of others?

4) How does one put together the demands of God for mercy, compassion and love of neighbor as self, with the human requirements of public safety and accountability before the law? Apply your responses as personally and specifically as possible.

5) Jesus identifies himself with those who are poor, suffering, being treated unjustly and imprisoned, telling us what we do to them we do to him. Practically, how does a Christian live this every day? How should Christians apply this to the justice and penal systems which act in their names?

V—CHANGING LENSES [1]

"An essential part of the Christian message is the concept of forgiveness, mercy and healing leading to reconciliation. This is what Jesus won for the human family on the Cross. These gifts form an essential part of what followers of Christ must practice in any age under all circumstances. They are among the most difficult of all virtues to practice. Practice entails the changing of peoples' hearts from anger, bitterness, hurt and resentment to hearts of compassion, healing and mercy. At the end of such a pathway lies true reconciliation...

"...From a Christian perspective no criminal justice system can afford to be built upon a philosophy of retribution, focusing primarily upon punishment flowing from feelings of revenge; a negative philosophy will produce negative results.

"Furthermore, an adversarial system by definition does not seek always to find the truth of a particular matter, but rather seeks a victory for one or other party. Such a system does not encourage offenders to take personal responsibility for their actions and can leave victims feeling that they are on trial too...

"We challenge this philosophy of retribution on the basis that it is negative and usually counterproductive. We believe it to be contrary to the example of Jesus in the scriptures and to the teachings of the Church. It attacks the very hope and possibility of conversion that the resurrection of Jesus seeks to proclaim."(Catholic Bishops of New Zealand)[2]

*   *   *

"I don't want your brother to die and I will do everything in my power to prevent it," were the words Bud Welch spoke to Timothy McVeigh's sister, Jennifer, while they cried together and he held her face in his hands. Welch's daughter, Julie, was killed in the Oklahoma City bombing. "I can tell you the rage and revenge I had after the Oklahoma City bombing was incredible." But, "I changed my mind about the death penalty. I know what temporary insanity is—I lived it."[3]

*   *   *

"'Forgiveness is hard work. Anyone who thinks forgiveness is for wimps hasn't tried it.' Marietta Jaeger should know. She makes herself pray each day for one good thing to happen to the man who kidnaped, raped and murdered her daughter. A founding member of Murder Victim Families for Reconciliation, she says, 'There's no one who can say to me, "Well, Marietta, you wouldn't be opposed to the death penalty if it happened to your little girl"... No amount of retaliatory death will compensate for the loss of our loved ones or restore them to our arms. And, in fact, to say that the execution death of any one malfunctioning person will bring justice is an insult to the immeasurable value of our loved ones' lives.'"4

*   *   *

The manner in which Bud Welch and Marietta Jaeger have chosen to respond to the terrible crimes committed against them challenge us to wonder if we would be capable of similar magnanimity. "Turning the other cheek" and "praying for those who persecute you" are extremely difficult. It is easier to understand the rage and desire to hurt back which, if left to fester, become spiritual cancers. Very often it is religious faith which plays the key role in gradually changing "the sword into a plowshare," converting the desire for blood into a commitment to till the soil for a fruitful harvest. Welch and Jaeger have *chosen* to see through very special lenses.

*   *   *

"Recent research has shown that people who are deeply and unjustly hurt by others can heal emotionally by forgiving their offender," says Robert Enright, a developmental psychologist at the University of Wisconsin at Madison. "Enright defines forgiveness as 'giving up the resentment to which you are entitled and offering to the persons who hurt you friendlier attitudes to which they are not entitled.'"

Enright explains that those who refuse to forgive remain in the power of the offenders. A Chinese proverb captures this truth: The one who seeks revenge should dig two graves, one for the person he will not forgive, the other for himself. Emotionally, forgiveness given to another is also a gift of healing to one's self. Studies show that those who are able to forgive were "less depressed and anxious, slept better, and were free from obsessive thoughts and revenge fantasies."5

*   *   *

Crime is committed by persons against persons—a fundamental concept of restorative justice—but the peace and harmony (shalom) of the families, friends and communities of both victims and offenders are disrupted, too. The pursuit of true justice requires that the needs and claims of all those affected be considered—including the offender's—and that all be involved in the process of restoring what has been shattered.

Our retributive justice systems are focused on the past and determining guilt. What happened and who did it are more important than what can be done to solve the problems created by the crime. "In the legal system, offenses and questions of guilt are framed in terms much different from how the victim and the offender actually experience them."

Even if the offender committed the crime, he may not be legally guilty. "Even if he is legally guilty, his attorney will likely tell him to plead 'not guilty'…In legal terms 'not guilty' is the way one says, 'I want a trial,' or 'I need more time.' All of this tends to obscure the experiential and moral reality of guilt and innocence."[6]

Our retributive system creates a game of "catch me if you can," in which the victim is mostly left out, while the offender is discouraged from acknowledging responsibility. The game ends when one side is able to claim, "I win! You lose!" The possibility of a "win-win" solution is not considered.

A primary obstacle to individual restorative responses, and to the restorative involvement of persons and communities secondarily affected by crime, is our adversarial justice system which relegates to the role of spectators even those most directly affected by the crime. Our systems and presumptions about justice also need to see through different lenses. The challenge to us as "the People" is to open the eyes of our hearts and minds to different ways of pursuing and measuring what it means to do justice.

Many local communities and a few states have begun to experiment with new visions and new goals. Just as new wine cannot be successfully stored in old wineskins, restorative justice models require the ability—and willingness—to see both the injustices and limitations inherent in retributive systems, as well as new possibilities for addressing crime in ways which not only punish, but also contribute to healing, reconciliation, restitution and positive personal and communal change.

Christians have been given the gift of Jesus, the Holy Spirit and the New Testament through which their vision can be checked and new lenses prescribed. Catholic Christians have the added rich treasures of the church's social justice and moral teachings to help focus how they see. And, Christians whose "eyes are sound" become sources of light to help others see more clearly.[7] Because of our faith in God's restoring redemption on our behalf through Jesus, we Christians have a distinct obligation to proclaim, practice and promote restorative justice within the civic communities in which we have been placed by God as "leaven"[8] and "salt."[9] We may not always "see eye to eye," but seeking the guidance of the Holy Spirit, as we search for new and better ways to do justice, we should have a compelling vision to offer our communities. If not—if we see through the same lenses as those who advocate merciless and vindictive "eye for an eye" justice—then what distinguishes us from those who do not know Jesus? Haven't we, in fact, become "the blind leading the blind?"[10]

Restorative justice visions and models are also found in abundance in the Jewish Scriptures and in the traditions of many indigenous peoples, including our own Native American nations. Changing lenses for most of us really means rediscovering our spiritual and cultural roots.

*   *   *

Charles W. Colson (sentenced to prison as a result of Watergate, and now, as a reborn Christian, leader of Prison Fellowship ministries) tells of his visit to Humanita Prison in Sao Jose dos Campos, Brazil. The former government prison has become an alternative prison run without armed guards or high-tech security. There are only two full time paid staff for the 730 inmates, serving time for everything from murder to drugs. Inmates do all the work, and the rules are based on love of God and respect for each other. Each inmate is assigned an outside mentor who works with him in prison and after release. Classes are offered on character development, and inmates are encouraged to take educational and religious classes. Humanita Prison has a recidivism rate of 4%, compared to 75% for Brazil as a whole.

The once infamous isolation cells used for solitary punishment now house only one inmate. "…my inmate guide put a key into the lock….and slowly swung open the massive door, and I saw the prisoner…a crucifix, beautifully carved—Jesus, hanging on the cross. 'He's doing time for the rest of us,' my guide softly said.'"[11]

*   *   *

The Vision of Restorative Justice

"Restorative justice is a philosophy that embraces a wide range of human emotions, including healing, mediation, compassion, forgiveness, mercy and reconciliation, as well as sanctions when appropriate. It enables the best virtues of human interaction to occur. Needless to say these are also Christian values. It also recognizes a world view that says we are all interconnected and what we do, be it for good or evil, has an impact on others.

"…The process provides the opportunity whereby those affected by criminal behavior—be they victims, offenders, the families involved or the wider community—all need to have a part in resolving the issues which flow from the offense. Victims and offenders assume central roles and the state takes a back seat. The goal is to heal the wounds of every person affected by an offense. No easy task, but surely a more honorable aim than merely focusing on punishing the offender."[12]

In restorative justice models, **crime** is focused upon from the perspective of the harm that has been done to persons and relationships (both individual and communal), rather than as violation of abstract law with the State as "victim."

The pursuit of **justice** has as its goals:

1. To identify the needs for healing and restitution which have arisen because of the crime.

1. To identify the obligations which have to be fulfilled.

1. To establish the process through which responsibility and accountability are clearly owned.

1. To facilitate and mediate the healing and restitution, and to determine what, if any, punishment "fits the crime."

In restorative justice models, the primary parties are the victims and offenders. Representatives of the community and court officials assume a supportive role in the process, and an ongoing role to assure accountability is honored.

Accountability is commonly understood as making sure offenders are punished for their offenses. Yet, "Without an intrinsic link between the act and the consequences, true accountability is hardly possible. And as long as consequences are decided *for* offenders, accountability will not involve responsibility.

"In order to commit offenses and live with their behavior, offenders often construct elaborate rationalizations for their actions…They find ways to divert blame from themselves to other people and situations…they work to insulate themselves from the victim…Many, if not most, offenders end up feeling that they have been treated badly (and they may well have!). This in turn helps them focus on their own plight rather than that of the victim…Consequently, offenders rarely are encouraged or allowed to see the real human costs of what they have done…

"[The offender] must be encouraged to develop as complete an understanding as possible of what he has done (i.e., what his actions have meant to the other person involved, and to acknowledge his role in it). He must also be allowed and encouraged to make things right to the extent that it is possible to do so. And he should participate in finding ways that this can be done. That is real accountability."

Without real accountability, neither the victim nor the offender can come to real resolution. Prison will only further debilitate the offender and magnify what is already dysfunctional in him. He will have no way to deal with his guilt, no opportunity to experience forgiveness, no chance to try to make things right. "In any case, he will continue to be defined as an offender long after he has 'paid his debt' by taking his punishment. The hatred and violence bred in him in prison may come to replace any sorrow and grief he may have had."[13]

Rather than creating an adversarial climate of "the People" vs "the criminal," restorative justice never loses sight of the reality that both victim and offenders belong to "the People."And, while neither the crime nor its consequences are minimized, the desired outcome is not ostracism and vengeful punishment of the offender to prove the triumph of good over evil. The restorative way begins with the harm done in the past, but measures its success by the good done for the future.

*   *   *

Over and over in the New Testament, Jesus models restorative justice. Many references have already been cited in the previous chapter, but the story of Zacchaeus is another occasion in which Jesus challenges us to change lenses and to comprehend the healing justice of God.

Zacchaeus was an outcast in his community. As an agent of the Roman occupation forces, he used his position to enrich himself at the expense of his neighbors. When Jesus comes to Jerico he invites himself to stay with Zacchaeus. The "good people" are scandalized, "…they begin to grumble saying, 'He has gone to the house of a sinner.'" Zacchaeus knows how unworthy he is, yet the unmerited respect with which he is being treated convicts and converts his heart. "Behold, half of my possessions, Lord, I shall give to the poor, and if I have extorted anything from anyone I shall repay it four times over." Zacchaeus has accepted responsibility for his sins against his neighbors, and has offered to make restitution at a level way beyond what the letter of the law might require.

The judgment of Jesus is, "Today salvation has come to this house because this man too is a descendent of Abraham." Jesus affirms Zacchaeus' rightful reintegration into the community, saying to the crowd, "He, too, is one of 'the People.'" And Jesus proclaims both the dynamic and goal of God's justice, "For the Son of Man has come to seek and to save what was lost."[14]

*   *   *

Whereas our traditional justice model relegates **victims** to bystanders, whose needs for healing, and whose own insights into what would help make things right, are mostly not heard or considered, in restorative justice models the victims and their needs and insights become the first priority.

Victims are allowed to be directly involved in every step of the process, and, if they choose (and the circumstances allow it) to enter into face-to-face dialogue with the offender. Whether through direct or indirect contact with the offender, the feelings and thoughts of the victim are sought out, conveyed to both offender and court, and seriously weighed.

Our failure to take the needs of victims seriously leaves a heavy legacy of fear, suspicion, and guilt. It leads to demands for vengeance. The demand for retribution may itself grow out of victims' failure to have a more positive experience of justice. Without a true experience of justice, neither closure nor healing come easily.[15]

Offenders learn the impact and harm their actions have caused to real persons and the community (as opposed to having violated a law). They are listened to respectfully, allowed to express their remorse and accept responsibility, and to be part of the process of determining just restitution and their role in restoring shalom. (If there is no acceptance of responsibility or remorse, then the traditional legal processes are followed. Restorative models cannot work in the case of denial of guilt, or a lack of desire to be part of the healing.)

As part of this process, the needs of the offender are also identified, as well as an understanding of factors which contributed to the criminal actions. And when punishment is determined to be appropriate, it is applied with a "medicinal purpose: as far as possible it must contribute to the correction of the [offender]."[16] Another goal of the restorative process is to provide support and resources to assist the offender in healing, rehabilitation and ultimate full reintegration into the community.

The **community**—represented by family members; police; religious, civic, business, labor and other groups; governmental and social agencies—are actively involved in whatever ways they can assist the victim and offender in healing the harm done, providing ways in which restitution (such as community service) can be fulfilled, and in offering practical services (such as counseling, drug treatment, job skill training and placement).

The active involvement of community members allows the communal dimensions of the harm done to be expressed, as well as the community's responsibility to assist the healing and restoration to be accomplished. This involvement strengthens the community by building bonds and networking, and exposing areas which the community needs to address in corrective and preventative ways.

The roles of **prosecutors** and **judges** are not eliminated in restorative models. The entire process is under the jurisdiction and supervision of the court, but the time spent in the courtroom is minimal, since most of the process is done in mediation and related contexts.

*   *   *

Not every crime, nor every offender is suitable for a restorative resolution. Not all victims are capable of, or open to, the process. An important initial role of prosecutors and judges is discernment. But, where restorative models are available and restorative values are the preferred goals of the justice system, even the traditional legal processes will be changed by the changed lenses and world views of those involved.

In our present retributive system, "Prison is not a sentence of last resort which must be justified and rationalized by the judge which imposes it. On the contrary, prison is normative, and judges find it necessary to explain and rationalize a sentence other than prison. This presumption of prison explains why our incarceration rates are so high."[17]

While restorative models work most easily in juvenile cases, misdemeanor and property crimes, the only limitations to what crimes can be handled in this manner are the limitations of the persons most directly involved. As Bud Welch and Marietta Jaeger give witness, some of us are capable of rising to amazing levels of forgiveness and compassion in spite of terrible injustices and harm done to us.

*   *   *

"Too often justice in society is understood as 'the vindication of individual rights'—to be achieved through court decisions and legislative action. Such an approach leads to 'unbridled affirmation of self-interest,' at the expense of others' interests.

"But justice in the biblical sense involves 'the restoration of right relationships'…and promoting 'connections rather than confrontation'…If we spend time, if we give time…there is created a sense of internal cosmos in which everything is connected, everything is centered, everything is seen in its proper light."

"If different sides keep talking and trying to relate on a personal level, 'some form of a just society may develop.'"[18]

*   *   *

Polls taken among those who have participated in restorative justice processes rank "holding the offender accountable" as their primary goal, followed by "providing restitution" and "making the victim whole." "Punishing the offender" was rated relatively low.

"Accountability means offenders take responsibility for their acts and take action to repair the harm to their victims and the community.

"To many, offenders being held accountable in the current criminal justice system means simply 'taking your punishment.' The victim and offender are put in passive roles while the 'system' tries to deal with the crime." The traditional system focuses on what is bad about the offender, and the actual harm done to the victim is not necessarily directly addressed.

"Accountability in restorative justice is based on the belief that when an offender commits an offense, the offender owes a debt to the victim and community. The two main ways an offender can be accountable are to honestly understand the impact of his or her behavior, and to take action to make things right and repair the harm…financial loss, hurt and anger, or a general loss of sense of security. The key to the process is that the harm is in concrete, real terms…Victim and community restitution is the norm—not the exception.

"This accountability also positively impacts the offender by offering"…increased hope of living up to one's potential…assistance in rising above past behaviors and in coming back into the community as productive members…"Rather than dwelling only on how 'bad' the offender is, restorative justice separates the offending person from the offense…by acknowledging strengths of the offender…ability to make amends is encouraged."[19]

*   *   *

"In St. Benedict's rule [500 AD] we find the practice of isolating the wayward monk in his cell, restricting his daily provisions and providing spiritual counsel. The idea was to allow time, silence and prayer to nourish the soul with the belief that one day the erring brother would rejoin the community's life.

"Monastic prisons were common and provided an effective antidote to civil society's brutal, public punishments…in 1704 Pope Clement XI built St. Michael's prison in Rome, incorporating many features of the monastic practice. It became one of the principal models for the development of prisons throughout the world."[20]

America's first prison was built by the Quakers at the end of the 18th Century as a humane alternative to corporal and capital punishment, which were the previous options for punishing crime. The goal of the first prisons was the restoration of offenders to society through work, Bible study and penitence (hence "penitentiary").[21]

Now, 200 years later, nearly 6 million Americans are incarcerated, on probation or on parole. We are in a period of overcrowded prisons; a binge of constructing new ones; the beginning of a privately built, owned and operated prison industry; and an emerging prison-industrial complex of private businesses and powerful correctional officers' unions, which **need** a growing number of inmates. So, political pressure grows for longer sentences and tougher parole conditions, as prisons absorb an ever increasing share of tax dollars at the expense of schools, parks and highways.

For the most part, the goals of rehabilitation and restoration have given way to prisons which are little more than human warehouses within which offenders languish for years, with little or no effort made to address the root causes of their dysfunction. Presently, in California 74% of parolees fail, and repeat the meaningless, dead-ended, expensive cycle of debilitation and dehumanization.

Our present approach to "corrections" is broken, rudderless and as morally bankrupt as are the treasuries of the states and local communities which are spending more and more on justice and corrections, and getting less and less of them. There are other, better ways. There have to be.

In Summary—Retributive and Restorative Assumptions

Retributive Justice	Restorative Justice
Crime is an act against the State, a violation of a law, an abstract idea.	Crime is an act against another person or the community.
The criminal justice system controls crime.	Crime control lies primarily in the community.
Offender accountability defined as taking punishment.	Accountability defined as assuming responsibility and taking action to repair harm.
Crime is an individual act with individual responsibility.	Crime has both individual and social dimensions of responsibility.
Punishment is effective. a. Threat of punishment deters crime. b. Punishment changes behavior.	Punishment alone is not effective in changing behavior and is disruptive to community harmony and good relationships.
Victims are peripheral to the process.	Victims are central to the process of resolving a crime.
The offender is defined by deficits.	The offender is defined by capacity to make reparation.
Focus on establishing blame, on guilt, on past (did he/she do it?)	Focus on problem solving, on liabilities/obligations, on future (what should be done?).
Emphasis on adversarial relationship.	Emphasis on dialog and negotiation.
Imposition of pain to punish and deter/prevent.	Restitution as a means of restoring both parties; goal of reconciliation/restoration.
Community on sideline, represented abstractly by State.	Community as facilitator in restorative process.
Response focused on offender?s past behavior.	Response focused on harmful consequences of offender?s behavior; emphasis on the future.
Dependence upon proxy professionals.	Direct involvement by participants.

Source: Adapted from Zehr, 1990 (See endnote #1)

Discussion Guide—Chapter V

1. On a personal level, how do you respond to the author's challenge, "If Christians advocate merciless and vindictive "eye for an eye" justice, then what distinguishes them from those who do not know Jesus?"

2. Restorative justice creates a context wherein all those affected by crime behavior—victims, offenders, families of both, community—have a part in resolving the issues which flow from the offense. If restorative justice were to become the norm, what positive or negative consequences would you foresee?

3. Restorative justice approaches crime from the perspective of the harm done to persons and relationships, rather than as a violation of a law with the State as victim. What positive or negative aspects do you find in this approach?

4. What place, if any, should retribution (punishment) have in our criminal justice system? Why?

5. Using the comparison chart on the last page of the chapter, which basic assumption of restorative justice most appeals to you? Why?

6. As a result of your reading and reflection, what, if any, "change of lenses" do you feel taking place within you?

VI—THE BETTER WAY

One of the young men of the Dakota tribe had been murdered. His enraged family members gathered to plan their revenge. As they vented their anger and spoke passionately of this insult to their family's honor and pride, the eldest—a man of great wisdom and influence—listened. Then he repeated what he had heard and affirmed its validity. Then he said,

> *"And yet…there is a better way. That the fire of hate may not burn on in his heart or ours, we shall take that better way. Go now to your homes…bring here the thing you most prize—a horse, say, or weapons, or wearing apparel, or a blanket. Easy ways and empty words may do for others…let us take the harder way, the better way…*
>
> *"The gifts you bring shall go to the murderer, for a token of our sincerity and our purpose. Though he has hurt us, we shall make him…(a relative), in place of the one who is not here. Was the dead your brother? Then this man shall be your brother. Or your uncle? Or your cousin? As for me, the dead was my nephew. Therefore, his slayer shall be my nephew. And from now on he shall be one of us. We shall regard him as though he were our kinsman returned to us."*

After some murmuring and inner battles to overcome their anger and injured pride, the family accepted the challenge

> *"because they saw that it was right. They saw that it was easy enough to fight violence with violence. Killing was the work of a moment. But to take the murderer as a relative, after what he had done, and to live in sincerity and creative good will with him, day in and day out to the end of life—that was something else."*

When the day came to confront the slayer, the family gathered in the council tepee. The elder offered the peace pipe to the murderer of their brother, son, nephew, and said,

> *"Smoke, with these your new kinsmen here. For they have chosen to take you to themselves in the place of the one who is not here…It is their desire that henceforth you shall go in and out among them without fear. By these presents which they have brought here for you, they would have you know that whatever love and compassion they had for him is now yours, forever."*

The slayer—now kinsman—was deeply moved and began to weep. He had been convicted by a love and compassion he knew he had no right to expect. Ultimately, "he proved himself an even better kinsman than many who had right of birth, because the price of his redemption had come so high."[1]

*   *   *

One can only pause in reverential awe after listening to such a story. Inside us there is a murmuring as the Great Spirit whispers to our spirits, "You are capable—and called—to the higher, better way."

*   *   *

"In 1980, when Catherine Blount and Eric Hanson were murdered by Douglas Scott Mickey, the loss of Catherine became what her mother calls her family's 'point of reference'—'All family history was prefaced as happening either before or after Catherine's death.'"

Eight years later, through her religion, Gayle Blount was able to forgive in her heart, and four years later she was able to write to express her forgiveness directly to Mickey, "This does not mean that I think you are innocent or that you are blameless for what happened. What I learned is this: You are a divine child of God…The Christ in me sends blessings to the Christ in you."

"From death row, Mickey replied, 'The Christ in me most gratefully accepts and returns blessings…to the Christ in you.'" He went on to say that through his own religious study he had come to understand the intensity of her pain. 'I would gladly give my life if I could change that horrible night.'"

It took Ralph Blount until 1996 to come to terms with his inner struggle for peace. He wrote to Mickey, "These negative feelings of hatred are not doing anyone any good; they serve no purpose; they have absolutely no influence on your life and they are in total opposition to Christ's teachings on forgiveness." Mickey wrote back to apologize.[2]

Gayle Blount has since visited her daughter's murderer several times, and become a vocal opponent of the death penalty. Both of Catherine's parents say they will ask for clemency when Mickey is scheduled for execution.

*   *   *

International attention focused on Laramie, Wyoming, in October 1998, after Aaron J. McKinney and an accomplice lured Matthew Shepherd from a bar and drove him out of town, where they tied him to a fence, savagely beat him and left him to die, because he was a homosexual.

Matthew's parents stunned the courtroom, where a jury was preparing to decide whether to impose the death penalty. Many wept as Matthew's father, Dennis Shepard, spoke of his son as a person who could only see good in others, and who had been "my hero," now gone forever, who "paid a terrible price to open the eyes of all of us" to the intolerance faced by the gay community. Then turning to Matthew's killer, he said, "Mr. McKinney, I give you life in memory of the one who no longer lives."

Judy Shepard, Matthew's mother, had initiated the agreement for a life sentence without possibility of parole. Since her son's death, Mrs. Shepard has become a human rights activist. Said Albany County prosecutor Cal Rerucha, "They lost what was most important to them, but they could look in the eyes of the man who took their son and give him mercy."[3]

The way of the Dakota family, the Blounts and the Shepards is harder because it challenges us to respond from the depth of the best of who we are, that depth from which the presence of the Divine within is activated not only through our professions of faith, but also by the painfully difficult decisions to trust, risk and live in faith. It is harder because it allows us no refuge from "them," as we reach out to embrace as kin, even those who have unjustly and grievously injured us, and, by doing so, offer them—and ourselves—redemption and hope.

With various motivations—from spiritual to fiscal—more and more individual citizens, professionals in justice and penal fields, religious and human rights organizations, political leaders and communities are seeking—if not the harder way—at least a better way.

*   *   *

The transition from retributive to restorative ways of seeking justice—the better ways—begins with a philosophical reorientation—a change of lenses.

Freeing ourselves from the locked in limitations of, "But we've always done it this way!," allows the possibilities of, "If we can dream it, we can do it!" There are many practical reasons for changing our approaches to criminal justice. The most universally accepted are that what we are doing now isn't working, and it is costing way too much humanly and financially. There are also more noble reasons for seeking change, including the conviction that all of us—victims, offenders, community—are "family," and that healing and restoring need to be our first priorities in doing justice.

Changing the ways we see and think takes time. Changing systems to implement new visions and new approaches takes time. It would be a mistake to suddenly lurch in a new, untested direction. Fortunately, much of the groundbreaking has been done through the studies of Howard Zehr and many others, and the experimental models already in place in many jurisdictions. But the *commitment* to a better way is the first and indispensable step forward.

*   *   *

"It is time for Californians to take a step back from the urge to incarcerate, take a look at the ongoing and projected costs of locking up so many people for non-violent and victimless crimes, and think about moving in the other direction. The evidence that throwing more people in jail really reduces crime is shaky at best, non-existent at worst—and the cost to taxpayers continues to spiral.

"It's time to think about ways to reduce the prison population rather than working to increase it."[4]
(Editorial, Orange County Register)

"I am here for an alcoholic problem which is curable. Yet I must face a long prison sentence…Our system for punishment is hideously archaic, abusive, and frightening, and it does nothing at all to restore human beings. In fact, it only festers more brokenness and breeds more crime. The women I am locked up with are displaced, homeless, abused, and uneducated. The system keeps them in that 'prison' by treating them as stupid and worthy of further degradation. This is the great evil that our society inflicts upon helpless women. We need to make these abuses known so that the system will take a hard look at where the real crime lies."[5]
(Jean, Los Angeles County Jail—Twin Towers)

*   *   *

What might happen if redemptive intervention, restorative diversion and broad community liaison became the normative *first option* for police and prosecutors. What if criminal prosecution and incarceration became the last resort?

In our civil law, we already have a system which defines wrongs in terms of injuries and liabilities rather than guilt. The desired goals of civil law are settlement and restitution, not punishment.[6]

If crime harms people, then criminal justice should be the search to make things right between people. Instead of defining justice as punishment, we will define it as restoration. The first goal of justice, then, ought to be restitution and healing for victims. The second major goal should be the healing of the relationship between the victim and the offender. Other goals will be healing and reintegration of the offender into the community, and acknowledging and attending to injuries done to the community.

Applying the biblical approach to restorative justice, we will seek to go beyond the original state of things in a transformative way to make them even better.[7] "We can denounce crime more effectively by doing things *for* the victim (and requiring the offenders to do so), rather than *against* the offender."[8]

*   *   *

Japan utilizes parallel systems—one similar to ours, one using the restorative justice approach. Cases move back and forth between them depending upon the nature of the crime and the nature of the offender. Also important are the offender's willingness to acknowledge guilt, express remorse and make compensation, **and** the victim's willingness to receive compensation and to pardon.

Whereas our adversary system discourages guilt acknowledgment, in Japan it is normative, and, once it happens, the focus becomes how to correct the injury. When the victim and offender agree to a just resolution, punishment is usually lenient. Long term imprisonment is used only for the most unusual cases. Japan has a very low crime rate, but a very high rate of conviction.[9]

When pain and long term imprisonment are inflicted, they should be our last resort and done with a sense of failure, rather than as the triumph of justice.[10]

*   *   *

Since 1989, New Zealand's juvenile justice system has been totally focused on restorative justice philosophy and practice for youth under 17. A parallel traditional system continues to handle cases of those who plead not guilty. All juvenile custody facilities have been closed, except for a few for youths who commit horrendous crimes, but the emphasis even in them is education, skill development and therapy.

There has been a considerable reduction in most categories of juvenile crime, and in the number of youths re-offending. The government is now seeking funding for pilot restorative justice programs for adult offenders.[11]

*   *   *

California's first victim/offender mediation program started in Fresno County in 1983. Presently, the program is experimenting with "a pilot program in which...non-violent juvenile felons will be sentenced at conferences that will include their families, teachers, neighbors, co-workers, members of their churches, probation officers, and those whom their victims want to invite."

The group's task "is to work out a sentence that makes things as right as possible with all concerned—victim, offender, community."[12]

*   *   *

Sacramento County has a dozen "neighborhood accountability boards," made up of volunteers screened by the Probation Department to sentence first-time juvenile offenders in non-violent misdemeanors. Contracts are drawn up; those who do not sign are sent to court for disposition. The "sentences are tailored not to the offenses, but to the youth's needs…The terms are designed to reinforce the positive influences in their lives."

Of the first 270 youths who have completed sentences through neighborhood boards, only 15 have offended again.

A 1995 Tennessee study of 241 similarly mediated cases showed recidivism cut by half compared to those processed through traditional sentencing.[13]

*   *   *

Sacramento City Police have just begun their Youth Intervention/Redirection Project for youths age 11 to 17 who have been arrested for petty theft. The youths and their parents are referred to this alternative to the juvenile court by their Neighborhood Accountability Boards as young people discerned with H.I.V. ("Hood Infected Virus") but who can be turned around before full-blown A.I.D.S. ("Addiction to Incarceration and Death Syndrome").

The youths and their parents (other family and friends are welcome) must attend a series of workshops on violence prevention, job skills, teen pregnancy and parenting, drug and gang awareness.

One of the officers involved said, "We're not just here to put them in jail. Our No. 1 goal is that [they] do not re-offend."[14]

*   *   *

Santa Clara County's pilot Restorative Justice Project is centered around Gilroy. "This project is about personal support and intervention. It puts faces on the victims and encourages offenders to take steps toward positive change."

Thirteen-year-old Anthony Alvarez was headed for the lockup after he and two other boys attacked a fourth. The straight A student never saw juvenile hall or a courtroom. He was given the option of enrolling in the project, and a panel of local residents "sentenced him to 10 hours of community service, counseling and a jail tour. In addition, the county offered to pay for three months of Karate lessons." A counselor made weekly visits to Anthony's home to keep track of his progress and school work.[15]

*   *   *

Sacramento County Juvenile Court Judge James Morris presides over Peer Court in which students from Cordova and Natomas high schools sit in judgment on students from other schools charged with vandalism and assault. "The crimes are real, the sentences are real, the consequences are real."

"Jurors cannot order the youths incarcerated, but they can render sentences ranging from community service to victim restitution to work-project participation."

The teenage court officers receive eight hours of professional training for their roles in the process. Plans are to implement the project countywide, and to include drug, shoplifting, drunk-in-public and other offenses. "Convictions are wiped off defendants' records if they commit no more offenses by age 18."[16]

*   *   *

Texas has pioneered a program dealing almost exclusively with violent offenders (half murderers). Its focus is serving the victims' needs. "The offender must admit guilt and take responsibility for his crime, and his treatment by the criminal justice system cannot be affected by participating. Victims and offenders undergo six months to two years of preparations…before they are brought together with trained mediators." Both sides share feelings and answer questions, and sometimes an "affirmation agreement" comes from the sessions in which the offender takes on a personal way of expressing remorse or making restitution.[17]

*   *   *

Minnesota's Carver County Sheriff's Department and Woodbury Police Department use Family Group Conferencing before or after sentencing in juvenile court, or as an alternative to it. The process brings together victims, offenders, the families of both, and other community members or resource persons to talk about how the crime has affected their lives, and to decide how the harm done might be repaired.[18]

*   *   *

The Crime Repair Crew of Dakota County, Minnesota, calls offenders who have been sentenced to community service to scenes of property crimes to fix and clean up the damage. The crew allows offenders to give back to the community for harm they have done, allows victims, offenders and other community members to meet in a restorative context, and offers offenders some training in construction and painting skills.[19]

*   *   *

All Victim/Offender Reconciliation Programs (VORP) have three foci in common: facts, feelings, agreements. The role of third party mediators is very important, but they try not to impose interpretations or solutions.

Through these programs, offenders come to know those they have harmed as real persons. They have their rationalizations confronted, and learn first hand the consequences of their actions. Because victims, offenders and the community work together toward resolution, all feel empowered, and are able to finish the process feeling justice was done, and that it was fair. Because of this, the possibility for reconciliation is also opened.[20]

*   *   *

What might be possible if judges worked closely with other government agencies, as well as community organizations and churches, to actively involve "the People" in the process of finding appropriate restorative responses for the unique circumstances of each case, and the special needs of the persons involved?

Yolo County Superior Court Judge Donna M. Petre received the 1998 Foundation for Improvement of Justice award for her leadership in revamping the way family-related cases are processed.

In 1997, civil domestic violence and guardianship cases were brought under family law. In 1999, juvenile cases were added. The goal is "to identify families that have multiple cases in their judicial system and deal with their problems as a whole…it is not uncommon to have a child in juvenile hall for delinquency, his parents getting a divorce in another court, a father whose criminal case is in another court and a second child who is a habitual truant and is before another court."

Judge Petre says, "At some point we have to say these are not defendants…This is a family that needs attention given to them in a unified way."

In addition to the consolidation, the courts have also established partnerships with various community social services agencies.[21]

*   *   *

In Manhattan's misdemeanor arraignment court, "those who plead guilty are sentenced and begin serving sanctions the same day. Aimed at low-level offenders, the court is designed to send a dual message…there are consequences for criminal behavior and that offenders must repay the community…that there is help for those who need it."

"A few repeat offenders go to jail, but most are sentenced to community service...Depending upon the offense, misdemeanants may be sentenced to participate in social services programs or may take part voluntarily" [long-term drug treatment, counseling, English as a second language class, high school equivalency class], and are escorted immediately to them. "A court-based social worker keeps track of the person on a daily basis. Offenders appear before the judge every two or three weeks where a case manager reports to the court on the person's progress."[22]

*   *   *

"Attorney General Janet Reno, condemning the failure of current criminal justice policies, called [Aug. 10, 1999] for a potentially radical restructuring of local court systems across the United States to prevent convicts from shuttling in and out of prisons 'again and again and again.'"

Reno's proposal would establish special courts in which judges would assume many tasks commonly associated with parole officers. Each judge would be empowered to oversee inmates' reintegration into society, and supervise their work, education, treatment and other programs. "Let's give our courts, our judges what it takes to do justice, what it takes to solve the human problems that bring the cases before them. It makes no sense to send someone to prison for armed robbery and have them come out in four years...without the problem being addressed."[23]

*   *   *

What positive new possibilities might emerge if legislators and governors exchanged the blinders of "tough on crime" for restorative lenses, and began to envision new goals and results for the criminal justice systems, and supported community-based sanctions whenever possible?

The Dakota family's choice for "the harder, better way" offers us an invitation to learn from the experiences and models of many of our Native American communities, many of which combine, in various ways, contemporary American approaches to justice with traditional tribal ways.

Customary law and practices are applied to:

Family Forums and talking circles presided over by family or community elders to resolve problems of interpersonal transactions: family or marital conflicts, juvenile or parental misconduct, assaults or property disputes.

Community Forums (similar to Family Forums) allow for the mediation services of village or tribal officials.

Traditional Courts handle criminal, civil, traffic and child welfare matters, and are presided over by heads of tribal governments, but maintain meditation processes in which the defendant and his/her family participate.

Some tribes have adopted contemporary American court models presided over by law-trained judges or lay judges, but there are common features in indigenous justice systems:

1. Non-adversarial, mediation approaches seek to discover the underlying problem(s) contributing to the crime or misconduct.

2. Offenders "remain an integral part of the community because of their important roles in defining the boundaries of acceptable and unacceptable behavior. Their actions are viewed as the result of natural human error that requires corrective intervention by elders."

3. Family and community input is sought and valued.

4. "Spirituality and use of tribal ceremonies are paramount."

5. "Restorative justice requires the offender to engage in activities that demonstrate his or her willingness to restore the relationship," such as cleansing ceremonies, counseling by the elders, sanctions of community service, restitution, temporary or permanent banishment.

6. "Sanctions are used to help the offender make amends, restore self-respect and dignity, correct behavior and heal the soul…"

7. "Reparative justice involves apology by the offender and forgiveness by victims, "as part of the process of safeguarding against vengeance and promoting harmony in the community.

Linkages are made to community, legal and social services to meet the comprehensive needs of offenders, victims and families."[24]

*   *   *

Other community-based sanctions recommended by California's Little Hoover Commission for lowering both recidivism and costs of criminal justice more effectively than incarceration:

Community Residential Restitution Centers provide 24-hour supervision of nonviolent offenders for 3–12 months. May require earnings to be given as restitution, as well as community service. Can offer education, employment services, substance abuse treatment.

Intensive Supervised Probation of weekly contacts between offender and probation officer. Can include treatment, counseling, educational or vocational training, restitution, community service.

Day Reporting Centers require daily contact with case managers who monitor community service, employment endeavors, etc., and which provide on-site programs.

Residential Treatment Centers for substance abuse and mental illness. Offenders may be confined to up to two years.

Also electronic monitoring, fines, community service and work release programs.[25]

*   *   *

In January 2000, 224 men and women in Sacramento County were serving home detention sentences for nonviolent drug and alcohol related convictions in lieu of being in jail. Participants wear an electronic ankle bracelet that emits a signal to a box attached to a phone at the inmate's home. The tamper-proof bracelet notifies authorities if the inmate wanders beyond 150 feet, although it also can be programmed to allow time for commuting to work, or attending substance abuse programs. Breath analyzers can also be attached to the phone to monitor alcohol use.

"In some cases, if you put someone in jail, they will lose their job and their home life. That can only exacerbate problems…," says Sacramento Superior Court Judge Gary S. Mullen. Says inmate Elena Teresa Contreras, "It enables me to work, to be with my kids at home so that I can continue to do my job as a parent. I get counseling and I serve my time."

Compared to $62.50 to house someone in county jail for a day, the county pays $8.00 for a home detention device, of which participants repay $6.70 plus one hour of their hourly wage each day.[26]

*   *   *

California's Department of Corrections operates six family facilities in which children to age six are able to live with their mothers. "The idea is to stop the intergenerational cycle, so the problems aren't passed on to the kids," says Sterling O'Ran of CDC.

To be eligible, women must be serving less than a five year sentence in a state prison for a nonviolent crime. They must agree to a rigorous schedule of drug counseling and parenting classes. Twice a month, groups of three or four mothers are allowed a four-hour outing with their children to a park or museum. Women who abuse the outings or fail to keep the program requirements risk being returned to prison. "There are a lot more challenges here," says Gina, who has been reunited with her 3-year-old daughter, Rayna, after 14 months apart. "You can't just think about yourself. If you break enough of the rules, you go right back, but you don't want to do that to your baby. You've got to stick with it."

While their mothers take classes or do chores, the younger children are cared for in the facility day-care center, while the older children attend neighborhood schools. Ninety women are currently in the six facilities: Oakland (2), Salinas, Norwalk, Pomona, Bakersfield. Two new facilities are scheduled to open in 2000, including one in San Diego, and an alternative program in Santa Fe Springs allows mothers to report directly with their children, instead of being sent to prison.[27]

Placing all inmates as close to their families as possible, needs to become policy for the good of inmates, their children and families—and the communities, which suffer from broken homes and delinquent children.

*   *   *

California's Office of Criminal Justice Planning has grants for two pilot juvenile violence courts. Thirty juveniles will be selected for the first year, and will be supervised by the same probation officers. The youths will receive intensive counseling and education, and will appear in court for monitoring at least once a week.

Superior Court Judge Thomas E. Warriner, who will preside says, "There's no silver bullet for solving these kinds of problems, but I think it's good the government is willing to give a good shot…for kids who want to change, this will allow them to."[28]

*   *   *

President Bill Clinton visited Watts during his 1999 summer campaign to encourage increased commitment to job training, education and economic empowerment of poverty areas of the country.

It costs an average of $25,000 to incarcerate each of the many young men who leave Watts for prison. Most of them are the result of one or more contributing factors: single-parent families, education failures, lack of employment, lack of hope for their futures, drug and/or gang involvement.

For every 100 men sent from Watts to prison, the state "invests" $2.5 million for their warehousing per year. What might be different if that money were invested in addressing the contributing causes instead?[29]

*   *   *

U.S. Supreme Court Chief Justice William Rehnquist, Attorney General Janet Reno, drug, "Czar" General Barry McCaffrey, and many judges and advocacy groups are calling for "a reassessment of mandatory minimum sentences that have incarcerated more than half the inmates in state and federal prisons for nonviolent offenses not involving major drug dealing."

Arizona and Missouri are among the states moving from automatic incarceration of drug offenders to "catch them, treat them and test them "approaches." "The idea is not be soft on crime but smart on corrections," says Missouri State Senator Harold Caskey.

Commissions have been established to rethink criminal codes in Arizona, Connecticut, Michigan and Oklahoma.[30]

*   *   *

Drug courts divert offenders "by staying either prosecution or sentencing while the person completes a year-long treatment program closely monitored by a judge."

Chair of the California Drug Court Project, San Bernardino Superior Court Judge Patrick Morris: "Drug court works better than voluntary clinics because the clinics don't have the incentives available and the person has the same old habits and the same old friends. We've always known that treatment works probably 7–1 over law enforcement, but the problem has been keeping the offender pinned to treatment. In drug court they go to the program just to avoid a prison term, but the program finally makes them look at themselves and by the mid-point they are moving on their own."

A federally funded study "found that recidivism among drug court participants ranges from 5 percent to 28 percent and drops below 4 percent for drug court graduates. That success record compares to a 45 percent recidivism rate among drug offenders who do not receive treatment."[31]

*   *   *

Arizona was the first state to direct all nonviolent drug offenders into treatment programs rather than prison. At $16.06 per day for intensive supervision and drug treatment, as contrasted to $50.00 per day for incarceration, the state saved $2.5 million in 1998.

Says Judge Judy Gerber of the Arizona Court of Appeals, "It was like a turnstile. Many of us came to the conclusion that we were parading through the courts and prisons without solving the root problems."[32]

*   *   *

In 2000, New York became the first state to require that nearly all nonviolent criminals who are drug addicts be offered treatment instead of jail time. Chief Judge Judith Kaye estimates the new policy will decrease the state's prison population 10%, with an annual savings of $500 million in prison, foster care and mental health costs, without requiring more beds in treatment programs.

"To be eligible, offenders would have to test positive for drugs and be willing to plead guilty. They would be assigned to specially trained judges who would monitor their cases. Instead of going to jail, the defendants would enter a rigorous treatment program and submit to strict monitoring by court officials. If they relapse, they would go to jail, most likely receiving stiffer sentences than normally given now..."[33]

*   *   *

"California's abysmal failure to fund community mental health programs is directly related to the increasing number of seriously disturbed people in our jails and prisons. Consider these shameful facts: 7.2 percent to 15 percent of county jail inmates statewide suffer severe mental illness...Eight to 15 percent of state prison inmates suffer severe mental illness...The overall costs of arresting, adjudicating and punishing Californians with severe mental illness is estimated to be between $1.2 billion and $1.8 billion a year."

"Everyone close to the problem—psychiatrists, social workers, families of those with severe mental illness and police—know that the mentally ill don't belong in our jails and prisons."[34]

*   *   *

Sacramento County has established a trial "project aimed at reducing crime and the revolving-door incarceration of mentally ill offenders, who make up at least 18% of the jail population." The pilot program is being supported by a state grant.

The program includes 100 misdemeanor offenders, and offers housing assistance, mental health and substance abuse treatment, transportation and other support assistance, and 24-hour support from case managers. "To measure effectiveness, the study group will be compared with 100 other inmates receiving traditional mental health services in jail during the same period."

Says Sacramento County Supervisor Roger Dickinson, "It's apparent that those suffering from a mental disability don't belong in jail. Being in jail doesn't do them any good."[35]

In September 2000, the Legislature expanded the program from 3 to more than 20 counties. Sponsor of AB 2034, Assemblyman Darrell Steinberg (D-Sacramento) said that whereas the state budget includes $55.6 million for the expansion, the program has already saved the state more than that. "We know that these services work and are worth replicating."[36]

*   *   *

The National Institute of Justice reported in May 1997 that benefits of using intermediate sanctions, as opposed to incarceration, justify the marginal increase in public safety risks:

> *"Intermediate sanctions can deliver much more intrusive and burdensome punishments than standard probation…can be much more punitive than probation and can be scaled in severity to the seriousness of the crime…Intermediate sanctions with strong treatment components can improve treatment effectiveness and thereby reduce recidivism rates."*[37]

*   *   *

In 1997, California prisons held 13,000 felons whose most serious crime was drug possession, and 6,700 whose crime was petty theft with a prior.

"Academic criminologists…overwhelmingly argue that the resources, responsibilities and strategies for punishing and converting criminals into law-abiding citizens are too focused on incarceration."

For over a decade, the Blue Ribbon Commission on Inmate Population Management has repeatedly reported that the "state strategy was too focused on prisons, where not enough is done with inmates to prevent them from committing new crimes once released…County programs, meanwhile, where there is the opportunity to help low-level criminals straighten out and avoid future crimes and convictions that will lead to state prison, had been starved for resources."

"The criminal justice system in California is out of balance and will remain so unless the entire state and local criminal justice system is addressed from prevention through discharge of jurisdiction."[38]

*   *   *

What if the money and resources invested were redirected from warehousing to addressing the root causes of crime and recidivism? Consider the potential benefit to inmates, the communities to which they will return—and the state budget—if the years spent incarcerated had a primarily restorative purpose of preparing offenders to return to society, rather than mostly a punitive goal?

A friend wrote from another prison, when he heard I was writing this book:

> *"You cannot come out dropping a lot of philosophical garbage on people each day about chang-*
> *ing their lives and showing them none of the material steps involved in that process, and think that*
> *they or you have made some great progress which will magically save them for the rest of their lives.*
> *Consider this, I sincerely desired to meet all these "philosophies," yet, in reality, I didn't even know*
> *how to go about getting a credit line going, how to get an apartment, how to get the phone or elec-*
> *tricity turned on, anything about insurance... all of these things do add to the frustrations and*
> *ultimate falls many experience... remember common sense things are not really common when you*
> *have no resources for* **immediate** *shelter, information, income..."*

Booker is not a philosopher, but a typical "Exhibit A repeat graduate" of our failed prison system. He was first incarcerated at age 9, and has spent 21 of his 38 years in and out of prison. Under "three strikes" the earliest he can hope to parole is 2032.

*   *   *

"I see 20,000 human beings locked up at a public cost of $22,000 a year each. And I say this is not working. Too many people are locked up who should be working and taking care of their families...We need to turn these bad guys back into good guys." With this rational and sensible assessment, Wisconsin Governor Tommy G. Thompson directed his corrections department to target funds "so that no inmate will leave prison without being able to read and fill out a job application."

The four-term Republican governor is also setting up workhouses for inmates with less than a year to serve, where they will do real private sector jobs, and be able to leave with proven skills and recommendations. "It's a way to rehabilitate, to re-assimilate them back into society."

First-time felony drug offenders (ages 17–25), who were not convicted of violence or gun use, get treatment, schooling and job training. "Then they get into a job with intensive probation to watch over them and make sure they are working. If we can get that dependency cured, it will be a huge gain for the state."

Governor Thompson notes that reforming the prison system's goals will not only cut state costs and help the economy by returning contributing workers and taxpayers, but also that "It's the right thing to do."[39]

*   *   *

"We can go on locking people up, but we have to start looking at the front end of the problem. We're fast becoming the No. 1 country for detention. We better start looking at kids. If you intervene at the earliest possible moment, you can reduce the number of people who wind up in the criminal justice system. The high chair, not the electric chair, is the answer."[40]

(George Sweat, Director, Office of Juvenile Justice, State of North Carolina)

When Sweat was Chief of Police of Winston-Salem, he practiced what he preaches. "My juvenile detectives had standing orders not to close a case without involving all the other agencies." (Schools, court, probation, private family service agencies.)

*   *   *

California's first serious commitment to prison drug rehabilitation began in Richard J. Donovan Correctional Facility in San Diego County. The program lasts 6–18 months in which prisoners spend four hours a day in intense group encounter sessions facilitated by a staff of ex-users, and continues with a support program after inmates are paroled. A study showed a recidivism rate of 16% for those who completed the aftercare program (as compared to over 70% system wide who were not in a rehab program).

About 80% of participants are coerced into the program by threat of loss of privileges. Interestingly, this group has a slightly higher success rate that those who volunteer.

As a result of the success of the program, Donovan's 300 beds committed to the program have been increased to another 1,400 at Corcoran. In 1998, 3,000 more were authorized, of which 600 have been activated in 200 bed programs at three other prisons. Each program costs about $750,000 annually. The amount being spent on the new prison (which will make no noticeable dent in the overcrowding) could have funded a new 400 bed drug program for one year in *each* of our 32 prisons.[41]

*   *   *

California's Proposition 36, passed by voters in November 2000, requires that, in most cases, anyone convicted of a first or second "nonviolent drug possession" offense be sentenced to probation and treatment, rather than incarceration. The state Legislative Analyst says this will divert at least 24,000 people annually from jail or prison at an annual savings of $200 million, and save the state an additional $500 million in capital costs for new prison space.[42]

San Francisco alone handles 8,000 felony drug arrests each year (60% of its caseload). The county cannot find treatment spots now, as is true throughout the state. Now, with six times as many placements needed, the state will need a crash effort to create, expand and license treatment providers. Says Barbara Broderick, Arizona's state director of adult probation, "Now that you have your law, you really have to embrace it and figure out how to make an incentive-based program work without the hammer."[43]

A 1994 Rand Corp. study concluded that "dollar for dollar, drug treatment here is far more effective in reducing cocaine use than going after street traffickers or chasing smugglers…an additional $34 million spent in drug treatment would reduce cocaine consumption in this country by 1 percent. In stark contrast, it would require $366 million to produce the same 1 percent reduction with local law enforcement and a whopping $738 million…with border interdiction and source country controls.[44]

*   *   *

Vice President Al Gore has proposed spending $500 million to help states test and treat drug addicts who pass through the criminal justice system. His "get clean to get out, stay clean to stay out" proposal is supported by many experts. White House drug czar Barry McCaffrey said, "Drug treatment is tough on crime because it stops crime." William Williford of the New York State Department of Correctional Services added, "Studies show it's about the best investment you can make right now in the criminal justice system."[45]

*   *   *

InnerChange, Texas' experimental prison pre-release program is "the nation's first 24-hour-a-day Bible-and-values-based pre-release program, aimed at helping inmates achieve spiritual and moral transformation."[46]

*   *   *

California's 1997 "Determinate Sentencing Act specifically abandoned rehabilitation as a purpose of prison and established punishment as the goal." "Because determinate sentencing defines the precise term an offender will serve… inmates and parolees have little incentive to cooperate in programs that might reduce their criminal behavior."

In 1995, the legislature directed the Department of Corrections to develop programs to educate and rehabilitate nonviolent first-time felony offenders. More recently, increased funding has been given to drug treatment programs. Nonetheless, programs and services provided are minimal, and less than 25% of inmates receive educational or vocational training that might help them after prison.

In 1997, 8% of inmates were in academic programs; 9% in vocational training; 4% in industry work. While the median reading level of state inmates is between 6th and 7th grad level, only 35–40% had access to literacy programs. "CDC has not put much effort into developing programs or encouraging outside providers to furnish services…even for inmates motivated on their own to take classes or learn a trade, opportunities are a catch-as-catch-can proposition… Inmates may spend an entire sentence on a waiting list…"[47]

State Senator Richard Polanco has sponsored legislation (SB 1845) that would create a new 15-member Correctional Education Board and superintendent appointed jointly by the Legislature, the governor, director of the CDC, and the chancellors of the University of California, California State University and California community colleges. The purpose of the bill is to create a structure—not under direct control of the custody structure—that can rebuild education opportunities in prison, and thereby improve public safety.[48]

*   *   *

Volunteers in Parole is a nonprofit group that matches attorneys and judges as mentors for parolees who have been discerned as most determined to change their lives. The program's goal is to break the "revolving prison door" syndrome. Mentored and employed parolees have a 70% success rate, compared to 29% for those who are not. The $50,000 annual budget pays for administration and transportation costs (twice as much for the entire program as it costs to house just *two* parolees returned to prison for failing parole!). A related tattoo removal project and scholarship fund are also in the works. Parolees selected for the program must be recommended by their parole agent, submit a written application and pass an interview. No one with violent or sex-related offenses is accepted.

The VIP program is sponsored by the State Bar of California and the county bar associations where the program is in place (Sacramento, Yolo and eight other counties presently), and is funded by the Department of Corrections Parole and Community Services Division. Over the past two years, 60 parolees have been mentored. At present, 23 lawyers and judges are volunteer mentors.

"A program like this bring the humanity back to the criminal justice system," says Yolo County Public Defender Barry Melton. Sacramento County Deputy District Attorney Tom Johnson says, "I'm not saying they should not have been sent to prison, but once they have served their time, they deserve help to reintegrate into society. I'm trying to help. One person at a time."[49]

*   *   *

"[A]s America's incarcerated population approaches two million, the value of imprisonment is a portrait in the law of rapidly diminishing returns. The justice system is becoming less capable of distributing sanctions and supervision rationally, especially where drug offenders are concerned. It's time for policy makers to change focus, aiming for zero prison growth."

"Spending on correctional institutions is crowding out spending on other proven crime-reduction strategies, including improved policing...in 1983, 52 percent of total U.S. criminal-justice spending went to police, 28 percent to corrections. By 1995, 43 percent went to police and 37 percent to corrections."

"The path to zero prison growth can be paved by five policy steps:

1). Repeal mandatory-minimum drug laws, release drug-only offenders and mandate drug treatment both behind bars and in the community."
2). "Reinvent and reinvest in probation and parole. Currently, we spend next to nothing on community-based corrections. We get what we pay for."
3). "Stop federalizing crime policy, and modify federal sentencing guidelines."
4). "Study and promote faith-based crime prevention and restorative justice...the best available empirical evidence suggests that religion significantly reduces crime and delinquency...Restorative justice returns America to the ethical understanding of those who founded the American penitentiary to reclaim public order and repair broken hearts, lives and communities on both sides of the walls."
5). "Redouble efforts at juvenile crime prevention."[50]

*   *   *

Drawing upon what I have read, heard from other inmates, and experienced firsthand of both prison and my companions here, I have come to some conclusions as to how prisons can be reformed and reorientated to accomplish the goals of enhancing public safety and cutting prison costs, while reducing future crime and recidivism. The pivot point for turning around the system is to refocus it on the restoration and successful reintegration of inmates into society. Changing directions will definitely require changing lenses on the part of the public, government leaders and corrections officials. But, what we have now is not working, and it is costing more and more to accomplish less and less.

Proposals for Restorative Directions in Criminal Justice

Introduction

Just as new wine requires new wineskins, it will be necessary to create new structures from the ground up to support new ways of approaching criminal justice reform. Much of the current mess is the result of piece-meal legislation, confused goals and expectations, overlapping areas of responsibility, lack of accountability, independent fiefdoms within the system (and within the same departments within the system) which do not communicate or coordinate. It will not be sufficient to simply rearrange the deck chairs on this lost and sinking Titanic.

What is essential now is a clearly defined overarching vision of the purposes and goals of the criminal justice and corrections systems (mission), and restructuring, re-staffing, retraining and re-legislating it into existence.

The lens through which to look into the future needs to be a restorative one. Each step of the process of rethinking and rebuilding needs to be tested by restorative questions and measurements.

A. Establish a Task Force on Criminal Justice and Corrections

1. Task

a. **Review** the present system (juvenile and adult)—prevention and intervention efforts, judicial processes, jail/prison, probation/parole, and administrative structures, laws, budgets, studies/reports/data—to gain an overview of the present status.

b. **Re-vision** a systemic restructuring with restorative goals to:
  (1) intervene at the earliest points to deter potential criminals and first offenders from entering the criminal justice system;

  (2) utilize an "it takes a village" approach by making it the norm to work in an integrated way with other government, community, private and religious agencies and resources.

c. **Propose** specific restructuring plans, goals and timetables for each component of the criminal justice-corrections system to:

2. Composition:

a. representatives of the governor, legislature, judges, attorney general, district attorneys, public defenders;

b. officials from the Department of Corrections, Youth Authority, parole, probation;

c. representatives of advocacy groups, religious and community organizations, education, addiction treatment programs, transitional support programs;

d.   former inmates, former prison administrators, former prison staff (psychologists, chaplains, educators).

B. The Court—A Restorative Team

1.   Minimize the adversarial nature of judicial proceedings to broaden the search for truth beyond determination of guilt, to an understanding of contributing causes, and toward seeking a response which will address the needs of victims, offenders and community in a healing way, including maximum flexibility for use of non-incarceration options.

3.   Provide adequate and real representation for offender and victims.

4.   Replace mandatory and determinate sentences as much as possible to allow maximum discretion for fitting the sentence to the unique situation.

5.   Create a new definition for "winning," to indicate a conclusion that does justice for victim, offender and community, helping restore all involved.

C. Prison

At present, all prisoners are treated alike. The primary factor in custody placement is security considerations. No attempt is made to discern those most likely to be "salvageable," or to place them in environments amenable to rehabilitation.

To move from simply warehousing inmates toward using incarceration for restoring and reclaiming as many as possible, a **two track prison system** will be necessary—one to support those trying to change, one for those who are not.

A thorough entry evaluation needs to be done for each inmate to determine special needs (such as education, mental illness, addiction), and his/her openness and potential for rehabilitation.

Each prison should specialize in responding to certain needs—such as educational and vocational training, or addiction or mental illness treatment—and have trained, competent staff to operate the programs. Inmates would be placed in a facility specializing in one or more of the areas of his/her determined need.

Inmates should again be eligible for Pell grants to allow those qualified to pursue college level education. Each prison would establish a contractual liaison with other state institutions and agencies, such as local colleges, to provide staff, credit and certification for educational and vocational programs, and, similarly, with employment, mental health and addiction treatment agencies for both in-prison services and post-prison assistance and monitoring. These programs need to be sufficiently independent to prevent their budgets and purposes from being compromised and subsumed by custody needs.

Track 1—Programming Toward Rehabilitation:

1. Each inmate begins with a program which he/she has helped determine. The program will have clear, achievable goals, and strict, continuous accountability monitored by frequent sessions with an assigned support counselor.

2. Program components might include: psychological counseling, education/vocational classes, addiction treatment, job, spiritual programs, family/parenting skills, health education, basic life skills, etc.

3. Maximum privileges are allowed.

4. Serious disciplinary problems, or failure to maintain program progress leads to transfer to non-programming track.

Track 2—Non-Programming:

The primary goal of this track is to motivate non-programming inmates toward programming by offering positive incentives for doing so, as well as negative consequences for not doing so.

1. These facilities would be maintained with minimal privileges, limited yard, TV and canteen access.

2. Optional self-improvement groups and literacy programs would be available, and recommendation by one of their staff members would be required to be considered for transfer to the programming track.

3. Every inmate would have an annual opportunity to be considered for transfer to the programming track.

Mandatory Pre-Parole Program:

Successful completion of this program would be required of **all** inmates prior to parole. Failure to complete the program would postpone parole.

1. The program would network with parole and community support programs to assure each parolee leaves with goals and a life plan; assistance in place for

housing and sustenance; contacts for continuing counseling, addiction treatment or education; job placement or training.

2. The program would offer training in survival and integrations skills, such as: money management, job hunting, interview and resume preparation, personal grooming and health, communication and conversational English.

D. Parole—Supervision and Support

1. Ideally, each county would provide a transitional halfway house option for parolees who lack a place to live, or a positive and supportive living environment. (Since 1998, the Legislature has been gradually increasing funds to provide or expand programs and facilities to assist paroles. The need, though, is vastly greater than the current resources.)

2. The primary focus of the parole officer (or a social worker partner) would be mentoring, supporting and supervising the implementation and progress of the reentry program.

    a) The parole officer would connect with the inmate and his/her pre-parole program prior to release to ascertain special needs, opportunities, problems.

    b) The parole officer would network with other government and community agencies and programs to connect the inmate to them.

    *   *   *

These are broad stroke proposals which need much refining and detailing. They are presented—from the perspective and experiences of an inmate—to begin the process of rethinking what is, and restructuring toward what might be a more effective system.

The initial financial investment needed to implement these proposals would be large, but, as with education reform, the long term benefits would more than offset the costs:

- saving individuals and families, and breaking the cycle of crime;
- changing tax-draining burdens on society into tax-contributing citizens;
- drastically cutting prison and corrections costs, thereby freeing funds for more productive civic needs.

I have become convinced by my experiences and studies that most parolees have a real chance to make it if sincere life-pattern changes are begun while incarcerated (e.g. educational, vocational, psychological), a strong spiritual foundation is in place, there is a realistic life plan (goals), and transitional support is waiting.

There are some inmates who will not change, no matter what efforts or systemic changes are made, but the goal of the system needs to be to reclaim as many men, women and youth as possible. Every effort should be made to support those who will succeed, if given the direction and support. Our corrections systems need to recapture **correction** as their primary mission.

There are inmates who are truly dangerous, who require special restrictive confinement, and should never be released, but they are few in number, and providing for their security requirements should not be the norm for the whole system.

And there are many who should not have been incarcerated in the first place, including those who are mentally ill, or addicted to drugs or alcohol. They need to be in specialized treatment facilities, which can treat the sickness rather than simply confine it while punishing the symptoms. Prisons have become our nation's substitute for effective policies on crime, drugs, mental illness, homelessness, poverty and illiteracy.

There will be nothing resembling justice—and there will be no peace in our communities—as long as we continue to return broken, dysfunctional, dehumanized, angry men and women back to our streets and neighborhoods after years of purposeless and directionless warehousing.

*   *   *

Reflections from
"Responsibility, Rehabilitation, and Restoration: A Catholic Perspective on Crime and Criminal Justice." A Statement of the Catholic Bishops of the United States, November 15, 2000.[51]

> *"Our criminal justice system should punish offenders and, when necessary imprison them to protect society. Their incarceration, however, should be about more than punishment. Since nearly all inmates return to society, prisons must be places where offenders are challenged, encouraged, and rewarded for efforts to change their behaviors and attitudes, and where they learn the skills needed for employment and life in community. We call upon government to redirect the vast amount of public resources away from building more and more prisons and toward better and more effective programs aimed at crime prevention, rehabilitation, education efforts, substance abuse treatment, and programs of probation, parole, and reintegration.*

> *"Renewed emphasis should be placed on parole and probation systems as alternatives to incarceration, especially for non-violent offenders. Freeing up prison construction money to bolster these systems should be a top priority.*

Abandoning the parole system, as some states have done, combined with the absence of a clear commitment to rehabilitation programs within prisons, turns prisons into warehouses where inmates grow old, without hope, their lives wasted.

"In addition, the current trend towards locating prisons in remote areas, far away from communities where most crimes are committed, creates tremendous hardships on families of inmates."
(Policy Foundations and Directions, #7)

＊   ＊   ＊

*"A Catholic approach begins with the recognition that the dignity of the human person applies to both victim and offender. As bishops, we believe that the current trend of more prisons and more executions, with too little education and drug treatment, does not truly reflect Christian values and will not really leave our communities safer. We are convinced that our tradition and our faith offer better alternatives that can hold offenders accountable and challenge them to change their lives; reach out to victims **and** reject vengeance; restore a sense of community and resist the violence that has engulfed so much of our culture."*(Introduction)

＊   ＊   ＊

There are other, better, more noble ways. Justice and peace *can* embrace.

Restorative Justice Signposts

We are working toward restorative justice when we…

1. focus on the *harms* of wrongdoing more than the rules that have been broken,

2. show equal concern and commitment to *victims and offenders*, involving both in the process of justice,

3. work toward the restoration of *victims*, empowering them and responding to their needs as they see them,

4. support *offenders* while encouraging them to understand, accept and carry out their obligations,

5. recognize that while *obligations* may be difficult for offenders, they should not be intended as harms and they must be achievable,

6. provide opportunities for *dialogue*, direct or indirect, between victims and offenders as appropriate,

7. involve and empower the affected *community* through the justice process, and increase its capacity to recognize and respond to community bases of crime,

8. encourage *collaboration* and *reintegration* rather than coercion and isolation,

9. give attention to the *unintended consequences* of our actions and programs,

10. show *respect* to all parties including victims, offenders & justice colleagues.

Crime wounds—justice heals

This page may be reproduced.

Harry Mika and Howard Zehr
Mennonite Central Committee
P.O. Box 500, Akron, PA 17501-0500
(717) 859-1151

Discussion Guide—Chapter VI

1) As you read the story of the Dakota tribe's surprising way of doing justice, what were your feelings? Your thoughts?

2) What is your answer to the author's question: "What might happen if redemptive intervention, restorative diversion and broad community liaison became the normative first option for police and prosecutors, and if criminal prosecution and incarceration became the last resort?"

3) Of the examples given of restorative justice pilot projects and policies, which one or two strike you as having special merit?

4) At the end of Chapter VI, the bishops give a summary of "*a Catholic approach*" to restorative justice. Even if you are not in full agreement, what do you find are the most compelling arguments for restorative approaches to justice?

5) If you were asked by a friend to briefly summarize what is meant by "restorative justice," what would you say?

6) The author proposes sweeping reforms to the justice and corrections systems. As a citizen and taxpayer, what is your reaction?

Taken from *Peace and Justice Shall Embrace* by A. Companion.
Published by Writers Club Press an imprint of iUniverse.com.

VII—LIVING STONES

"Driving home, I allow myself to cry the tears I held back at the prison in Chowchilla. I am haunted by the faces of the women standing at the small windows to their solitary confinement cells hopefully waiting for one of us to come and talk with them. No one calls out. Their lonely eyes are their call."[1]

(Sr. Suzanne Steffen, CSJ)

*　　　　　　　　　*　　　　　　　　　*

"Judges in our criminal courts need your prayers. There is a tradition in our church: on Sunday during prayer our minister specifies by name and title persons in high public office, and we as a church ask God's guidance for them as they formulate and administer public policies. For years my name has been on that list. I have felt the immense power of my church family praying for me weekly. It has buttressed my determination to hold fast for policies of hope, to pursue ideas not because they are popular but because they bring healing…Please pray for us."[2]

(Judge Patrick J. Morris)

*　　　　　　　　　*　　　　　　　　　*

Restoring justice and its fruits: peace, healing, redemption and hope, and restructuring the processes and systems of doing justice to foster restorative justice, require the committed involvement of people of faith and vision at every level—"it takes a village" to create a community in which justice and peace can embrace.

Christians, both as individuals and as church communities—with Jesus Christ as Cornerstone and the Holy Spirit as animator—are called to be "living stones" through which a community of justice and love is established.[3] It takes a whole church to **be** church: people of the pews, clergy and religious, bishops, diocesan departments, parish ministries, church organizations.

The Catholic Church, in particular, offers a long tradition of moral theology, and a century's worth of phenomenally inspiring and challenging social justice teachings.

Vatican II's constitution, *The Church in the Modern World*, strongly condemns the attempt to separate one's spiritual and religious life from one's social and vocational life as, "one of the most serious errors of our time." The Council warns that those who fail to integrate the two aspects of love of God and concern for neighbor into a holistic, living faith, "jeopardize their eternal salvation."[4]

The U.S. National Conference of Catholic Bishops has produced a rich treasury of social justice documents covering the full range of contemporary challenges and opportunities for building a society of peace and justice. As the bishops lament, "…far too many Catholics are not familiar" with these teachings, and "many Catholics do not adequately understand that the social teaching of the Church is an **essential** part of Catholic faith."[5]

The prophetic, countercultural stance of the Catholic Church in defense of the unborn has been—for far too many parishioners and preachers—a narrow, myopic proclamation and practice of the church's defense of human rights and dignity. Too often, the same voices who rightfully admonish Catholic politicians for their schizophrenic isolation of abortion as the one public issue over which their Christian conscience has no claim, practice the same circumscribed teaching and preaching on abortion, as though it were the only application of the church's respect for life commitment.

Many critics—both within and outside the church—understandably dismiss a human dignity agenda which appears to begin with conception and end with birth. Truth in advertising would require many Respect Life Committees to be renamed Anti-Abortion Crusades. Only a consistent, "seamless garment"[6] promotion of the totality of Catholic social teaching is truly Catholic (and catholic), and offers credible witness to our society of a "seamless Gospel vision" of how a just people create a just community with "justice and peace for all."

"Cafeteria Catholicism/Christianity" (a term used by some to disparage the genuineness of faith of those who seemingly pick and choose the teachings of the popes and bishops they consider binding) is not limited to issues of doctrine or discipline. The term could just as aptly be used for those who selectively pick and choose the social justice teachings of the *same* popes and bishops.

A Christian will always flounder for scriptural, doctrinal, moral or social justice underpinnings which leave any human person outside of the dignity of "child of God," or which will dispense from the bond of "neighbor" who has the claim of "brother/sister." The question is not, "Who has a greater claim to my love: the unborn child, the child in the ghetto, the grown-up child in prison, the victimized child, the elderly child terminally ill?" The question for Christians—because it is the question Christ asks—is, "How will you love *me*, minister to me, heal me, restore *me* in **each** of them, in **all** of them?"

*   *   *

"Principles, once internalized, lead to something. They prompt activity, impel motion, direct choices. A principled person always has a place to stand, knows where he or she is coming from and likely to end up. Principles always lead the person who possesses them somewhere, for some purpose, to do something, or choose not to."[7]

What, then, are the principles which undergird the Catholic social justice teachings which are to be accepted as an essential part of Catholic faith, which should be part of a well-formed conscience, and which should guide and determine our faith-in-action ministry?

While there is no official list of these principles, this synthesis by Fr. William J. Byron, S.J., draws from those articulated in various pastoral letters of the U.S. Catholic bishops and papal encyclicals. Not all of them are as immediately applicable to our focus on restorative justice, but each adds another nuance to the vision one should expect from those viewing life through Christian lenses.

Ten Principles of Catholic Social Teaching[8]

1. **The Principle of Human Dignity**
    "Every human being is created in the image of God and redeemed by Jesus Christ, and therefore is invaluable and worthy of respect as a member of the human family" (*Reflections*, p. 1).

    Simply being human establishes one's claim to human dignity and a place within the human family.

2. **The Principle of Respect for Human Life**
    "Every person, from the moment of conception to natural death, has inherent dignity and a right to life consistent with that dignity" (*Reflections*, pp. 1-2).

3. **The Principle of Association**
    "…the person is not only sacred but also social. How we organize society—economics and politics, in law and policy—directly affects human dignity and the capacity of individuals to grow in community" (*Reflections*, p. 4).

4. **The Principle of Participation**
    "We believe people have a right and a duty to participate in society, seeking together the common good and well-being of all, especially the poor and vulnerable" (*Reflections*, p. 5).

    All persons have a right not to be excluded from participating in those institutions which are necessary for human fulfillment.

5. **The Principle of Preferential Protection for the Poor and Vulnerable**
    "In a society marred by deepening divisions between rich and poor, our tradition recalls the story of the last judgment (Mt. 25:31–46) and instructs us to put the needs of the poor and vulnerable first" (*Reflections*, p. 5).

For the common good, preferential protection for the voiceless and powerless members of the community is necessary to keep society from dividing into the social unrest and violence which comes with "us" vs "them."

6. **The Principle of Solidarity**
"Catholic social teaching proclaims that we are our brothers' and sisters' keepers, wherever they live. We are one human family…" (*Reflections*, p. 5).

7. **The Principle of Stewardship**
"The Catholic tradition insists that we show our respect for the Creator by our stewardship of creation" (*Reflections*, p. 6).

8. **The Principle of Subsidiarity**
This principle puts a proper limit on government by insisting that no higher level of organization should perform any function that can be handled efficiently and effectively at a lower level of organization by individuals and groups closer to the problems and issues. (*Reflections*, p. 6)

9. **The Principle of Human Equality**[9]
"Equality of all persons comes from their essential dignity…While differences in talents are part of God's plan, social and cultural discrimination in fundamental rights…are not compatible with God's design" (*Summary*, pp. 23–24).

10. **The Principle of the Common Good**
"The common good is understood as the social conditions that allow people to reach their full human potential and to realize their human dignity" (*Summary*, p. 25).

Surely the common good is enhanced by criminal justice and penal systems which seek to restore offenders to positive and contributing roles within the community, and which foster the processes of healing reconciliation, which, in turn, promote peace and harmony.

                    *   *   *

The principles of social justice, as with the Gospels, Ten Commandments and the virtues, require personal and communal reflection and integration, out of which will flow just living and activity. Restorative justice is nurtured by the personal and communal witness and commitment to it.

There is a necessary and important role for every person and component of the church in promoting justice and peace: bishops, diocesan departments, parishes, parish organizations and ministries, church-connected organizations, ecumenical groups. All of these can give public voice and active support to forming the political climate for change through support of public officials working for just changes, and through advocacy efforts to inform and persuade others. Some individuals and groups are capable of direct involvement in ministering to victims and offenders, and to their families. Those parishes and dioceses in which jails and prisons are situated have a special responsibility to be actively involved in direct ministry to Christ in prison, and to support the ministries of detention chaplains.

Reflecting upon vignettes of my prison experiences, a priest friend wrote, "The worst prison of all is to not believe that God can change the human heart, and our ministering in that same spirit is hopeless. Without radical hope and love, we Christians have little to offer a world of calculated outcomes based on the weakest instincts of our human nature."

Below are some models, ideas, needs and possibilities for restorative justice ministry at every level of the church. Particular local needs, talents, inspirations and opportunities will offer others. The only limitations will be closed hearts and ears plugged to the cries of victims, offenders and their families, and to the promptings of the Holy Spirit. "Whoever has ears ought to hear what the Spirit says to the churches."[10]

*   *   *

Dioceses and Religious Communities

1. Establish, staff, fund and support jail/prison ministry as a diocesan department/community ministry, or as an office within Social Justice or Catholic Charities.

    1. At jails/prisons with full time or part time chaplains, support their ministries with funds, supplies, resource personnel and programs of diocesan offices, and provide training for volunteer and inmate ministers.

    2. At jails/prisons without full time or part time chaplains:

        a. Coordinate, train and resource efforts of volunteer priests, deacons, religious and laity in providing Mass/sacraments and pastoral care; provide training and resources for inmate ministers.

        b. Assist pastors of parishes in which there are jails/prisons in establishing detention ministry by organizing, training and resourcing.

        c. Promote jail/prison ministry at diocesan congresses, and by providing speakers for parishes, schools, church and civic groups.

d.   Provide a regular detention ministry column in the diocesan/community newspapers.

e.   Provide bulletin inserts for parishes, high school newspapers, church organization newsletters, and local media to educate and advocate.

f.   Advocate on behalf of victims, inmates and their families with local, state and federal officials and agencies.

2.   Network with other church, civic and government groups to:

a.   Support families of victims and prisoners;

b.   Provide opportunities for victim/offender reconciliation.

c.   Provide after-release assistance with housing, jobs, counseling and other practical needs.

3.   Establish liaison with police, district attorney, public defender, courts, parole office to offer involvement and church resources in support of restorative mediation, healing and reconciliation efforts.

4.   Sponsor and/or operate a transitional housing/reintegration facility for parolees, or take leadership in an ecumenical or total community effort to do so.

5.   Religious communities "adopt" one nearby jail/prison for personal visits, spiritual counseling, volunteering as chapel program sponsors or leaders.

a.   Older, infirm sisters/brothers, who are unable to visit, can adopt one or two inmates for a mail and prayer ministry.

*   *   *

Pope John Paul II asked the world's bishops to visit prisons during the 2000 Jubilee year. "Imagine what might happen if every bishop on earth…[visited]…at jails that even God seemed to have abandoned. Imagine the nuisance they would create for prison administrations, the sensation they would be for the media, the contempt they would meet from many prisoners, the solace and hope they might bring to others. Imagine all the bishops making this a worldwide topic of conversation and action…Then imagine what a difference the bishops could make together, a brand new collegiality. It would be a calamity if this inspired idea were allowed to fade."[11]

*   *   *

Bishop Daniel A. Hart (Norwich, Connecticut) says Mass at a prison and visits with inmates on a monthly basis. His diocesan offices minister to families of inmates.

*   *   *

In February 1999, Auxiliary Bishop Gabino Zavala (Los Angeles) led eleven Catholic leaders to the men's death row at San Quentin State Prison. This was only one of a series of visits organized by Bishop Zavala and the Detention Ministry Office of the archdiocese. Afterwards he said, "Society likes to lock these people up and forget about them, and Catholics do the same. That's not what we are called to do."

Reflecting upon the visit, Auxiliary Bishop John Wester (San Francisco) said, "You know, when you meet these men, they're real human beings. You see the whole issue of the death penalty is not just a theological moral debate. You're dealing with real people."[12]

*   *   *

"The gospel sounds radical and prophetic inside prison walls. Prison mirrors our culture, it teaches you all that is not right about it. Inside the prison, you see everything so clearly: the grave problems women and children face in our society, racism, the way we have eradicated community. Everything is about isolation, separation, division."[13]
(Sr. Suzanne Jabro, CSJ, Director, Detention Ministry, Archdiocese of Los Angeles)

*   *   *

Bishop Bernard W. Schmitt (Wheeling, West Virginia) has suggested the Catholic Church should consider running its own privately operated prisons, just as it has successfully done with schools and hospitals. (And as the church is successfully doing in Brazil and Chile.) "Maybe a more hands-on approach by the church would give it an opportunity to demonstrate its mission to heal, rehabilitate and socialize."[14]

Parishes, Church Organizations, Schools

1. Many of the suggestions listed above are applicable for implementation by parishes, church organizations and schools.

2. Parishes having a jail or prison within their boundaries have a special responsibility and opportunity to establish a detention ministry and to support the efforts of chaplains and the diocese.

    a.   Recruit and support volunteers for detention ministry.

    b.   Provide funds and spiritual resources (personnel and materials).

4. All parishes, through existing ministries and parish church-related organizations are able to:

    a.   Include victims, prisoners, their families and detention ministers in prayer intentions.

    b.   Include ministry to prisoners as part of respect life and social justice teaching and preaching.

    c.   Include detention related topics in parish bulletin.

5. Identify families of prisoners living within the parish and reach out to them by:

    a.   Inviting them to active parish involvement (perhaps through "adoption" by a family with similarly aged children or who live nearby, who will help them make connections and feel welcome).

    b.   Providing for special needs: practical assistance, counseling, Christmas toys, school scholarships.

    c.   Connecting with inmates who will be returning to the parish before their release (perhaps through the "adopting family" or a sponsor) to:

        1.   Let them know they will be welcome.

        2.   Anticipate reintegration assistance which will be needed, and to act as advocate/liaison in connecting to support services.

6. Identify appropriate community service work which would benefit the parish, and contact county probation to offer the parish as a resource for community service fulfillment.

7. In communities in which restorative mediation programs are being used, notify those in charge, as well as parishioners, of the availability of parish personnel to be part of the process.

        *   *   *

Fresno's St. Benedict Catholic Worker has established a ministry at Fresno County Jail. Catholic Worker community members make one-to-one visits to inmates, distribute Bibles and recovery literature, and work in partnership with St. John's Cathedral Parish to provide bilingual Mass and Communion services.

The steps of the jail are transformed "into a place of sharing, talking, praying, crying, laughing and loving," as Catholic Workers provide released inmates with snacks, warm clothes (in winter), change for phone calls and bus fare, as well as smiles and support, as they begin their challenging and scary return to society. "It brings hope and fellowship which keep the demons of despair and loneliness at bay."[15]

*   *   *

Resurrection Parish (P.O. Box 87, Aptos, CA 95003) has begun a parish-based ministry to the county jail, in which parish members lead Communion services and retreats, and adopt inmates as pen pals.

*   *   *

Larry and Diane Callahan of Sacred Heart Parish, Medford, Oregon, host a neighborhood Christmas social at their home each December. The event not only has built a friendly, caring neighborhood, but, coordinating with the county juvenile hall staff, the Callahans ask each family to bring a gift for a specific child.

*   *   *

Dominican Sister Dorothy Biggs of Medford, Massachusetts, has begun a campaign to get churches, convents, monasteries, synagogues, mosques and temples throughout the country to ring their bells for two minutes at 6 p.m. every time there is an execution anywhere in the country. (In the absence of bells, to hang a black drape.) Bishop Walter Sullivan of Richmond, Virginia, is among those who have joined the campaign.[16]

*   *   *

An associate of arts degree program is offered at San Quentin State Prison (the only such program in the state prison system) because of volunteer professors from St. Mary's College in Moraga, undergraduate students, student teachers, and donated texts and materials. The program was begun five years ago by Dr. Naomi Janowitz of the University of California, Davis, along with volunteer faculty from Davis and U.C. Berkeley. It is accredited through evangelical Patten College in Oakland.[17]

*   *   *

Since 1986, St. Raphael (San Rafael) parishioner Roberto Becerra has been a volunteer at San Quentin's Catholic Chapel. During his weekly visits, he listens to inmates who need someone with whom to talk, offers spiritual encouragement, interprets for Spanish-speaking inmates and prepares inmates for First Communion.[18]

*   *   *

Brother Modesto Leon, CMF, and the Los Angeles County Probation Department have opened the S.E.A. Charter Girls Academy to help reclaim girls who have had their first contacts with the criminal justice system, or are in danger of doing so. The academy offers an array of services: career counseling, job preparation, computer training, tutoring, pregnancy prevention, parenting classes, mentoring by older women, discussion groups on personal dress and decorum, self-esteem workshops, counseling. A plan is developed and monitored for each girl.[19]

*   *   *

A volunteer support group, Sister's Keeper Liaison, at Rio Consumnes Correctional Center in Sacramento County, offers support to women inmates, helps prepare them for reentry into the community, and connects them to support programs and practical assistance when they leave. The group's goal is to establish a half-way house.[20]

*   *   *

The Inside Out Network of volunteers from several parishes ministers to the inmates at Napa County Jail and Juvenile Hall and their families, with special attention given to the needs of Hispanics. Under the direction of Fr. Gordon Kalil, members of a Renew group in St. Apollinaris Parish began providing spiritual counseling. The program has grown to also serve as a bridge for inmates preparing to leave jail. The Network has one set of two-person teams meet with the women and men in jail and their families to learn what their needs are. A counterpart team assesses the information and helps make the contacts with service agencies, helping overcome obstacles such as language barriers, illiteracy and poverty.[21]

*   *   *

Our Lady of Guadalupe Parish in Soledad invited inmates at Los Angeles county Jail and Twin Towers I and II to submit their names for prayer. The names were inscribed on a huge scroll placed before the altar, and, during mass, the names were read out as parishioners prayerfully responded, "Presente!"[22]

*   *   *

Women Religious Advocates for Women Prisoners is comprised of representatives of nine congregations within the Leadership Conference of Women Religious—Region XIV (California). Their collaborative purpose is to raise awareness of women religious to the needs of women in prison in order to advocate for them and to work toward systemic change. The Advocates sponsor visits for sisters to women's prisons to acquaint them firsthand with both the inmates and prison realities. A pen pal project has evolved from the visitations, and a pilot program is under development to assist parolees, as they make the transition from prison.[23]

*   *   *

"Get On the Bus" brings children to visit their inmate-mothers on Mother's Day at Valley State Prison for Women in Chowchilla. Sr. Suzanne Steffen, CSJ, coordinates the event, which is a joint effort of the Los Angeles Archdiocesan Office of Detention Ministry, Justice Partners: Women in Criminal Justice, Center for Children of Incarcerated Parents, Costco and McDonald's. After initial skepticism, prison authorities have become enthusiastic supporters of the program.[24]

*   *   *

Kairos begins with a weekend retreat and a follow up monthly gathering at the Federal Correctional Institute for women in Dublin, California. Volunteer team members come to provide the ministry in support of chaplain Rev. Ronald Richter's efforts to provide a place "…where they can get in touch with their spirit to endure their sentence."

Team members do not try to develop personal relationships with inmates, but encourage and support their relationship with God. "Our real goal is to build Christianity inside the prison rather than just declare the gospel. You try to build an environment where you live it out."

Kairos is active in many prisons throughout the country. National headquarters are in Winter Park, Florida, Ike Griffin, Executive Director.[25]

*   *   *

Everyday of the week at Folsom State Prison near Sacramento, groups of inmates gather for centering prayer. The Contemplative Fellowship is a self-rehabilitation ministry run by inmates through the support of an outside sponsor. Felons from different ethnic and religious backgrounds meditate and pray together. The group has developed a library of books and cassette tapes, and has an outreach ministry in every housing unit. Group leaders claim a 0% recidivism rate of active members who paroled during their first three years.[26]

Individuals and Families

1. In parishes where the pastor and/or parish ministries are supporting jail/prison ministry, get involved in a specific way according to your gifts, time and circumstances:

    a. Volunteer as a sponsor or leader for a jail/prison prayer group, scripture study, religious education class, faith-based 12 Step programs.

    b. "Adopt" a family of a prisoner to provide personal and practical support.

    c. "Adopt" an inmate for personal visits, letters, care packages. (Before establishing contact with an inmate, or giving your home phone or address, contact: the prison/jail chaplain, Friends Outside Office, local prison volunteer, or your diocesan detention ministry office for advice and prison regulations regarding mail, packages and visiting.)

    d. Support a jail/prison chaplain or your parish detention ministry through fasting or tithing money, and/or crafts and materials (toys, rosaries, religious books).

    e. Advocate within your church and civic communities on behalf of victims, prisoners and their families, write legislators in support of restorative justice measures, consider detention related issues when voting for candidates.

    f. Include victims, offenders and their families, as well as officials responsible for doing justice in the community's name, in personal family and public prayers.

    *   *   *

Reflections from
Responsibility, Rehabilitation, and Restoration: A Catholic Perspective on Crime and Criminal Justice, A Statement of the Catholic Bishops of the United States, November 15, 2000.[27]

> "[N]ew studies confirm what our pastoral experience has demonstrated: that physical, behavioral, and emotional healing happens sooner and with more lasting results if accompanied by spiritual healing." (Offenders and Treatment)

> "The Church must stand-ready to help offenders discover the good news of the Gospel and how it can transform their lives. There should be no prisons, jails or detention centers that do not have a regular and ongoing Catholic ministry and presence. We must ensure that the incarcerated have access to these sacraments. We especially need to commit more of our church resources to

support and prepare chaplains, volunteers, and others who try to make the system more just and humane. We are grateful for those who bring the Gospel alive in their ministry to those touched by crime and to those in prison. The Church must also stand ready to help the families of inmates, especially the young children left behind." (The Church's Mission #3)

"*A primary role for the Church is to gather people of different viewpoints and help them to reach common ground. Out of this dialogue can come greater appreciation for diverse perspectives, credibility for the Church's involvement in the issues, and ultimately a change of heart and mind by those who can impact the criminal justice system so that it more fully reflects gospel values.*

"*We bishops encourage dioceses to invite jail and prison chaplains, victims of crime, corrections officers, judges, wardens, former inmates, police, parole and probation officers, substance abuse and family counselors, community leaders and others to listening sessions. The purpose of these sessions would be to gain a better appreciation of all the parties affected by crime and involved in the criminal justice system, to seek common ground on local approaches to crime, to collaborate more easily in areas of mutual concern, and to build community among all these people of goodwill who are trying to make society safer and life more complete.*" (Appendix, Organize Diocesan Consultations)

*   *   *

"*Dear Friends in Jail and Prison Ministry,*

As Chairman of the Prison Ministry Committee of the California Catholic Conference…I join with you as you share your gifts and talents, and the presence and compassion of Jesus Christ, with those…incarcerated in our detention facilities, jails and prisons. You are a faith filled community generously responding to the call to bring Good News to the poor, to proclaim liberty to captives.

"*I join with you also in the struggles of your ministry, especially working within the criminal justice and corrections system which so often fail to meet basic standards of justice for offenders, victims and society. Our standard of justice is God's justice, justice which restores and enhances the human dignity of each person, even the thief, the rapist, the kidnapper, the burglar, the drug dealer, the murderer, the person who does not 'deserve' justice. The justice you bring…as you attend to the spiritual, pastoral, sacramental and social needs of the incarcerated, embraces the forgiveness, healing and compassion of Jesus.*

"*Many want to permanently lock up or execute those you are called to serve, to love, to heal, to restore and to reconcile. I join with you against these prevailing social attitudes and* *values. I join with you to challenge our Church, especially those in leadership, to intervene and to confront, consistently and faithfully, institutions and systems that depersonalize, dehumanize and demoralize the human spirit and take away the human dignity to which **ALL** are entitled as God's children created equal in the image and likeness of God. Let us remember that Jesus often said to his disciples, 'do not be afraid,' and that he assured them, 'I am with you.'*

"Let us pray with and for each other, for the incarcerated and their families, and for victims of crime and their families. May the peace and compassion of Christ be with us all."

Most Rev. Gabino Zavala
Bishop, San Gabriel Pastoral Region

Discussion Guide–Chapter VII

1) Since social justice is an *essential* component of our faith, as our popes and bishops tell us, what evidence of working for social justice do you see active in:

   a) Your own life?

   b) Sunday homilies?

   c) Parish ministries and priorities?

2) What is your understanding of the "seamless garment" approach to respect life advocacy?

   a) Do you find this approach at work in your own efforts to promote respect for life?

   b) In your parish?

3) Which of the listed ten Principles of Catholic Social Justice do you personally find most challenging to live out?

4) In what specific ways could ministry to prisoners and their families be undertaken:

   a) By you and your family?

   b) By your parish, or church/community organizations?

Taken from *Peace and Justice Shall Embrace* by A. Companion.
Published by Writers Club Press an imprint of iUniverse.com.

VIII—PEACE AND JUSTICE SHALL EMBRACE

Once there was a man of great means—a King perhaps—who had two sons. One day the younger son came to his Father and demanded, "Give me my share of what will be my inheritance—now!" Whereupon he left home and soon squandered all his Father had given on partying and prostitutes.[1]

*   *   *

Once upon a time there was a handsome prince who had been placed under a curse and turned into an ugly frog. His only hope was to find a princess who would believe there was hidden beauty behind his ugliness and free him with her kiss.[2]

*   *   *

These two wonderful parables have fascinated me all of my life. Each speaks in symbolic ways of my experiences of myself, of how God has worked (and continues to work) in my life, of my sins and my redemptions, of the people with whom I have shared life. The stories touch core truths and realities of my story—every human story—and, in simple, inviting images expose the curses and their sources, and offer the hope and way of redemption.

The more I have reflected upon what is commonly know as the Parable of the Prodigal Son, and the more I have assumed the role of the prodigal, the more I have come to realize that I am also my brother, the other son.

Depending upon the moment in my life when I read the parable, and my degree of self-awareness, I am able to switch scripts, so that at one time I am the unfaithful and wayward son, at another time his faithful (albeit self-righteous and hard-hearted) brother. I also experience myself being and doing for others, as my Father does for me. At other times, I am sharing from the sidelines in the joy of the lost one returning home or restored to his rightful place.

Most of all, with the wisdom which comes only after brokenness and healing, I have come to understand that the primary story being told is that of my Loving Father. In spite of my wanderings, my Father has never disowned me.

*   *   *

When the son who has wandered comes to his senses—broke, hungry, hopeless, remembering how good it was at home—he turns his back on where he has been and begins the process—step-by-step-of returning to his Father. Jesus does not tell us he is sorry for what he has done, only that he "came to his senses." As he makes his way toward home he is fearful of how he will be received; he rehearses what he will say to his Father in the hope of tempering his just anger; he does not hope to be restored to his former position, but only that he will be allowed a cot in the servants' bunkhouse. He knows he is not worthy of anything more. He knows he has become ugly under his self-imposed curse.

All the time the prodigal has been gone, the older son has been his Father's obedient, faithful, dependable support. He has worked hard in his Father's fields, quietly and without asking for anything. He is the model son—at least until his brother comes home. When given the challenge to rise above his understandable resentment toward his brother for all he has done to hurt his family and increase his own workload, he shows his hidden ugliness, and unwittingly admits that he is in need of being kissed and redeemed, too.

We don't know how the elder son's story ends. Jesus leaves him standing outside the joyous homecoming feast, unable to even refer to his sibling as "my brother," and muttering in protest at his Father's incomprehensibly lavish welcome for "that son of yours!" In spite of his Father coming outside to find him and invite him in as well, the elder son is bent on holding onto his hurts and angers, and remains standing in the darkness outside the celebration. He protests his Father's refusal to mete out punitive "justice."

In their own ways, both sons show how they have taken their Father's love and goodness for granted, and how they have dissipated their rightful inheritance to all their Father is and has. Just as the older son is confused by the unmerited restoration of his brother, so the prodigal must also have been. He felt and saw himself as ugly, and that was reinforced by his older brother's incensed self-righteousness. Both were dumbfounded by the discovery that they were equally loved by their Father and embraced as sons. They each expected "justice," instead they experienced grace. They could not grasp what their Father was trying to teach and show them: "You are brothers! We are family! It cannot be 'us' vs 'them' in my house!" Perhaps they were not yet old enough to have learned how much of the one was in the other, and how much they were both capable of being in the image of their Father.

Would it have helped them, I wonder, if they could have watched their Father every day, as he stood at the window overlooking his land? If they could have felt the prayerful, searching, hopeful surveying of the horizon in the direction from which one son had disappeared from sight, but not from heart? Or, if they could have sensed the intensity of the pride and gratitude welled up in his heart as he regarded—through the same window—the tireless dedication of his son supervising the servants and gathering the harvest? Were they capable—are any of us—of truly believing that we are never out of our Father's vigilant affection, and that we are loved regardless of what we do or leave undone?

And, if we claim to understand and to accept what the two sons could not, are we equally able to commit ourselves to embracing the prodigals in our own families, among our own friends, within our own communities? Can we really trust that beneath the ugliness—our neighbor's and our own—that there is a child of the same Father—a prince or a princess in disguise. Are we willing to risk a restorative embrace?

Luke places the parables of the lost sheep, the lost coin and lost son immediately after Jesus admonishes the pharisees for their hypocritical and judgmental self-righteousness, and exhorts his disciples—as "salt of the earth"—to restore the potential of what has gone flat and seemingly become worthless.

*   *   *

Frog kissing requires honesty and humility regarding our own ugliness and unworthiness, otherwise the log of self-righteousness in our eyes narrows our vision so we only see the splinters in the eyes of others. Embracing prodigals is remembering-in-action how many times we ourselves have been embraced and welcomed home.

Ugly frogs plead with us, "Kiss me, I may be a prince!" Christians—remembering how their own ugliness was healed by God's redemptive embrace—respond, "I will, because I **know** you are!"

*   *   *

Pope John Paul II at Regina Coeli Prison, Rome, July 9, 2000:[3]

> *"[Catholics are to be] engaged for the dignity of all, a dignity that flows from the love of God for every human person."*

> *"[God calls you inmates] to walk a way of justice and truth, forgiveness and reconciliation. The jail from which the Lord comes to liberate you is, first of all, the one in which the spirit is chained. Sin is the prison of the spirit. God desires the integral liberation of man, a liberation that regards not only the physical and outer conditions of life, but which is in the first place a liberation of the heart.*

> *"The penal system cannot be reduced to a simple retributive dynamic or some sort of institutional vendetta. The pain inflicted by prison only makes sense if, while asserting the demands of justice and discouraging crime, it also serves the renewal of the inmate, offering the one who erred a chance to reflect and to change his life, and then to be reinserted into society with full rights.*

> *"Perhaps the ones to whom you caused pain will feel more justice has been done watching your interior conversion than simply knowing you have paid a penal debt."*

*   *   *

Working for the kind of peace which restores persons and communities, and heals hurts and estrangement, necessitates a commitment to an ancient-new vision of what it means to do justice. It will demand more than prayer from disciples of Jesus and others who envision a better, nobler way. It will take patient advocacy, leadership, prodding, witnessing.

Whenever I've seen the bumper sticker, "Envision World Peace," I've smiled and thought, "If only it were that easy!" Yet, there is real spiritual wisdom in that pleading appeal, because peace and justice are just as much a matter of attitude and vision, as a process. If I change the way I think, understand and value things to do with peacemaking and living justly, that will lead to a change of feelings and actions.

Then, if I join with others who are seeking to incarnate similar visions, we not only support and enhance each other's efforts, but we become the ministers of "Envision Peace" and "Do Justice," putting "bumper stickers" on the foreheads of legislators, the entrances to voting booths, the backs of church pews (and the front of pulpits and miters), courthouse steps and prison bars, school desks and family TV screens.

Justice = punishment, punishment = accountability, and accountability = incarceration is a discredited, dysfunctional, dead ended vision. There is a crying need for new visions, new lenses, new ways. Envision these headlines: "Victim and Offender Reconciled," "City Initiates Parolee Reintegration Program," "Local Parish Opens Halfway House," "Candidate Pledges to Work for Healing Instead of Hurting."

In your heart, in your home, in your parish, in your community, live and proclaim: **"Peace and justice shall embrace!"**

Discussion Guide—Chapter VIII

1) Share a personal experience of having been "redeemed"—accepted and loved in spite of what you had done and how unworthy you felt.

2) Briefly share how each of the two brothers in the parable, and their father, understand "justice."

3) Call to mind a recent media-sensationalized crime. Share your thoughts and feelings regarding the accused offender, victim(s) and other affected persons, as you became aware of the details of the crime, saw pictures of the people involved, listened to the comments of witnesses, police and others. Share how you found stereotypes, prejudices, retributive or restorative justice judgments influencing your thoughts and feelings.

4) What is the author saying?: "Frog kissing requires honesty and humility regarding our own ugliness and unworthiness…Embracing prodigals is remembering-in-action how many times we ourselves have been embraced and welcomed home."

5) What is your personal reaction to the hope the Pope offered prisoners?
"Perhaps the ones to whom you have caused pain will feel more justice has been done watching your interior conversion than simply knowing you have paid a penal debt."

6) Applying this statement to yourself, respond to: "If I change the way I think, understand and value things to do with peacemaking and living justly, that will lead to a change of feelings and actions."

Taken from *Peace and Justice Shall Embrace* by A. Companion.
Published by Writers Club Press an imprint of iUniverse.com.

ENDNOTES

Introduction

1. The Cypriot Embassy did not respond to my inquiry seeking to verify the accuracy of my memory, and to obtain names and dates.
2. John 8:1–11.
3. Howard Zehr, *Changing Lenses* (Herald Press, Scottsdale, AZ, 1990), pp. 87–91.
4. Isaiah 11 and 2.
5. Romans 5:8, 10.
6. Howard Zehr, pp. 139–140.
7. Howard Zehr, pp. 130-132.
8. Jeremiah 31:31-34; Hebrews 10:16.
9. Howard Zehr, pp. 181.
10. Psalm 85:11.

Chapter I

1. Luke 10:29–37.
2. Howard Zehr, *Changing Lenses* (Herald Press, Scottsdale, AZ, 1990), pp. 78–81.
3. Howard Zehr, p. 203.
4. Howard Zehr, p. 51.
5. "Rate of Felon Parolees Returned to California Prisons: Calender Year 1997," Dept. of Corrections, Administrative Services Division, Sacramento, Ref. No. PYRET-2, March 1998, Table l.
6. California Department of Corrections, Third Quarter Report 2000.

Chapter II

1. Jack Henry Abbott, *In the Belly of the Beast* (New York: Vintage Books–Random House, 1991), 112–122.
2. "Responsibility, Rehabilitation and Restoration: A Catholic Perspective on Crime and criminal Justice," U.S. Catholic Bishops, 15 Nov. 2000. Order from Publications Office, United States Catholic Conference, 3211 Fourth St., NE, Washington, D.C. 20017.
3. "Prison Numbers Over 2 Million," The Sacramento Bee, 10 Aug. 2000:A17.
4. "Violent Crimes Fall 10%," The Sacramento Bee, 28 Aug. 2000:A1.
5. Molly Ivins, "Corruption in the System," Tri-Valley Herald, Dec. 1998, and Edward Walsh, "1 in 150 Americans Behind Bars," Washington Post, as reported in The Sacramento Bee, 15 March 1999:A6.
6. Matthew B. Stannard, "Report: Jail Terms Increasing, The Sacramento Bee, 11 Jan. 1999, and Andy Furillo, "After Long Climb, State's Prison Population Declines," The Sacramento Bee, 6 May 2000:A1.

7. Steve Geissinger, "April 2001—No More Room At the Inn," The Sacramento Bee, 4 Feb. 1999:A4.

8. The Washington Post as reported in The Communicator (California Men's Colony, San Luis Obispo), Feb.-Mar. 2000:3.

9. Gerald F. Uelmen book review of *A Sin Against the Future* (Vivien Stern, Northwestern Univ. Press), America, 22 May 1999:34.

10. Ivins.

11. "Justice Jottings," newsletter of the Presbyterian Church (U.S.A.), Criminal Justice Programs, Summer 1996.

12. Carl McQuillion, "What's Up With Lifers?," The Communicator (California Men's Colony), July 1998.

13. Peter Blumberg, "Most Who Go Before Parole Board Find No Way Out," Los Angeles Daily Journal, 14 May 1999:1.

14. Dan Smith, "Davis Stealing Crime as GOP Issue," The Sacramento Bee, 19 July 1999:A1.

15. Editorial, "Politics of Parole," The Sacramento Bee, 14 Oct. 1999:B6.

16. "Davis, Parole Board Take Tough Stance on Early Releases," Associated Press as reported in The Sacramento Bee, 4 Oct. 1999:A4.

17. Blumberg.

18. Senate-New-Reply@sen.ca.gov, 20 Aug. 1999.

19. Claire Cooper, "Don't Mistreat Disabled, Parole Board Told," The Sacramento Bee, 23 Dec. 1999:A4.

20. Legislative Analyst's Office, "2000 Budget Analysis."

21 .Jon Matthews, "Prison-Building Funds Approved," The Sacramento Bee, 17 June 1999:A3.

22. Ted Strickland, "The Problem with Private Prisons," The Washington Post as reported in the Tri-Valley Herald, 26 June 1999.

23. National Catholic Reporter, 2 July 1999:32.

24. "Report: Prosecutors Suppress Evidence," The Sacramento Bee, 11 Jan. 1999:A16.

25. John Jacobs, "Prison Guards Find an Adversary in Lockyer," The Sacramento Bee, 20 July 1999:B7.

26. Nat Hentoff, "George W. Vetoes the Bill of Rights," The Sacramento Bee,11 July 1999: B7.

27. "In the Governor's Words," The Sacramento Bee, 2 Mar.2000:A15.

28. Herbert Sample, "Davis:Judicial Picks Should Follow My Wishes or Quit," The Sacramento Bee, 1 Mar. 2000:A1.

29. Bishops Jerry Lamb, Robert Mattheis, Melvin Talbert, "A Plea to Davis for Siripongs," The Sacramento Bee, 1 Feb. 1999:B5.

30. Dan Smith, "Clemency," The Sacramento Bee, 22 Jan. 1999:A1.

31. Fox Butterfield, "Inmates Serving More of Sentences," New York Times, as reported in The Sacramento Bee, 11 Jan. 1999:A6.

32. Leslie Wirpsa, "Trying to Make Justice Work for Women," National Catholic Reporter, 29 May 1998: 12–13.

33. Abbott, pp. 60-61.

34. Laura Mecoy, "LAPD Scandal Exposes Angry Rift Between Chief, DA," The Sacramento Bee, 16 Mar. 2000:A1.

35. Patrick Hoge, "New View of Police Excesses," The Sacramento Bee, 22 Mar. 1999:A1.

36. "Legislators Blast Prison Officials Over Brutality," The Sacramento Bee, 24 Oct. 1998.

37. Mark Arax, "New Complaints By Women Inmates Spur State Probe," Los Angeles Times as reported by The Sacramento Bee, 29 Oct. 1999:A7.

38. Claire Schaeffer-Duffy, "Long-Term Lockdowns," National Catholic Reporter, 8 Dec. 2000:3.

39. Elizabeth Olson, "From All Sides, U.S. Takes Heat Over Human Rights," New York Times, as reported in The Sacramento Bee, 28 Mar. 1998:A15.

40. Bob Egelko, "Kennedy Warning on Europe's Courts," The Sacramento Bee, 17 Oct. 1999:A4.

41. Nat Hentoff, "Accused Are Losing the Right to a Lawyer," The Sacramento Bee, 7 May 1998:B7.

42. "Sledgehammer Justice," The Sacramento Bee, 6 June 1998.

43. Janet Wilson, "Rally Calls Foul on 'Three-Strikes'," Los Angeles Times, 1999.

44. Wayne Wilson, "Jurors Booted for '3 Strikes' Objection," The Sacramento Bee, 2 Feb. 2000:A1.

45. Editorial, Los Angeles Times, as reported by The Sacramento Bee, "'3 Strikes' Strikes Too Hard," 29 Aug. 1999:I4.

46. "Swinging at Three Strikes," The Communicator (California Men's Colony, San Luis Obispo), Spring 2000:5.

47. "Campaign Aims to Reform '3 Strikes' Law," The Sacramento Bee, 23 Sept. 1999:A4.

48. Jon Matthews, "Study of '3 Strikes' Finds No Effect on Crime Rate," The Sacramento Bee, 9 Nov. 1999:A3.

49. Dan Walters, "Fact Irrelevant to Issues Game," The Sacramento Bee, 11 Nov. 1999:A3.

50. Kathryn Casa, "Prisons: the New Growth Industry," National Catholic Reporter, 2 July 1999:17.

51. John Cloud, "A Get-Tough Policy That Failed," Time, 1 Feb. 1999:48–51.

52. "A Bid to Ease '3-Strikes' Penalty on Lesser Crimes," The Sacramento Bee, 9 Apr. 2000:A1.

53. "Alcohol, Drugs Linked to 80% of Inmates in U.S.," The New York Times as reported in The Sacramento Bee, 9 Jan. 1998.

54. Cloud.

55. Cloud.

56. Marc Mauer, "Heavy Time for Crack Convictions," The Sacramento Bee, 9 Feb. 1999:B7.

57. "Drug Addiction is Treatable," The Sacramento Bee, 18 Mar. 1998:B10.

58. Patrick Hoge, "Shortfall in Alcohol, Drug Treatment Documented," The Sacramento Bee, 14 July 1999:A3.

59. Dan Smith, "Davis Kills No-Prison Plan for some Parolees," The Sacramento Bee, 8 July 1999:A3.

60. Editorial, "Maximum Exploitation," The Sacramento Bee, 20 Jan. 1999:B6.

61. Fox Butterfield, "Prisons Replace Hospitals For Nation's Mentally Ill," The Sacramento Bee, 22 Mar. 1998:Forum.

62. Patrick Hoge, "Hope on the Street," The Sacramento Bee, 14 Mar. 1999:A1.

63. Reynolds Holding, "State Prison System Settles Suit Over Disabled Inmates," San Francisco Chronicle, 13 Aug. 1998:A21.

64. Fox Butterfield, "Prisons' New Role: Mental Hospitals," New York Times as reported in The Sacramento Bee, 12 July 1998:A1.

65. Tammerlin Drummond, "Cellblock Seniors," Time, 21 June 1999:60.

66. Steven A. Capps, "Growing Gray tide Will Color Our Future," The Sacramento Bee, 27 June 1999:A1.

67. Bernard Star, "Releasing Aging Inmates Could Save Taxpayers a Lot," The Sacramento Bee, 17 Sept. 1999:B7.

68. Chris Schreiber, "Behind Bars," Nurse Week, 26 July 1999:10.

69. Drummond.

70. George M. Anderson, SJ, "Living and Dying Behind Bars," America, 29 May 1999:10.

71. Thomas C. Fox, "Texas, Belly of the Death-Penalty Beast," National Catholic Reporter, 12 Feb. 1999.

72. Joan Ryan, Columnist (newspaper source and date unavailable).

73. "Detention Ministry," Archdiocese of Los Angeles, June-August 1999.

74. "Youth Arrest Decline," The Sacramento Bee, 13 Dec. 1999:A1.

75. "Inmates: Juveniles Are 16, 17 Year Olds," Tri-Valley Herald, 15 Dec. 1999:1.

76. Lisa Greer, "Tough is Not Smart, When It Comes to Juvenile Crime," Restoring Justice (Archdiocese of Los Angeles), Spring 1998, Vol. 2, No. 2:1.

77. "Lock 'Em Up,' Time, 14 Feb. 2000:68.

78. Denny Walsh, "CYA Inmate Used As 'Concubine,' Suit Says," The Sacramento Bee, 8 Feb. 2000:A4.

79. Editorial, The Sacramento Bee, 6 Jan. 2000:B6.

80. Steven T. Jones, New Times (San Luis Obispo), 26 Apr. 1998:10.

81. "Prison Education," The Sacramento Bee, 12 Aug. 2000:B6.

82. "Beyond Bars," The Little Hoover Commission Report on Corrections in California, (660 J St., Suite 260, Sacramento, CA 95814), Jan 1998:4, 46–49.

83. California parole failure rates were 67% in 1996 and 74% in 1997, Dept. of Corrections.

84. Editorial, The Sacramento Bee, 23 Feb. 1998.

85. Andy Furrillo, "Tough Parole Board Chief Close to Ouster," The Sacramento Bee, 10 Mar. 2000:A1.

86. "Report on Corrections in California."
87. "Correction–News," June 1998.
88. "Report on Corrections in California."
89. Michael A. Kroll, "Violence Breeds Violence," Tri-Valley Herald, 1 Mar. 1999.
90. Howard Zehr, *Changing Lenses* (Herald Press, Scottsdale, AZ 1990) pp. 35–38.
91. Kroll.

Chapter III

1. John Paul II, Jan. 27, 1999, Trans World Dome Stadium, St. Louis, Missouri.
2. Patricia Lefevere, "Just Another Night on Texas' Death Row," National Catholic Reporter, 4 Feb. 2000:6.
3. Leviticus 20:10; 24:16.
4. Leviticus 24:17.
5. Leviticus 20:10; 24:16.
6. Leviticus 20:9; Exodus 21:17, Exodus 31:15.
7. National Catholic Reporter, 26 Mar. 1999:28.
8. "Death Penalty Cases Criticized," The Sacramento Bee, 15 Nov. 1999:A6.
9. "Critics Blast Defense Lawyers in Death Penalty Cases," Tri-Valley Herald, 6 Feb. 2000:16; "Illinois Governor Orders Hold On All Executions," 1 Feb. 2000.
10. "Execution Moratorium Picks Up Speed, ABA Says," The Sacramento Bee, 13 Feb. 2000:A6.
11. "Death Sentences Reversed," The Sacramento Bee, 3 June 2000:A1.
12. Morris L. Thigpen, "Indelible Imprint," The Other Side, Jan.-Feb. 1994:17–18.
13. Sara Rimer, "Justice Becomes Issue in Alabama Death Row Cases," The Sacramento Bee,1 Mar. 2000:A6.
14. David Kravets, "Two Decades Later, Child's Killer Still Awaits Execution," Ventura County Star, 20 Nov. 2000:A1.
15. Theresa Malcolm, "Tucker's Death Affected Robertson's Views," National Catholic Reporter, 23 Apr. 1999:4.
16. George W. Brooks, "Prison Ministry: To Free the Souls of Captives," U.S. Catholic Conference (Washington, D.C.): 1998.
17. Julia Alloggiamento, "Death Row Spiritual Advisors Face Resistance at San Quentin," Restoring Justice (Archdiocese of Los Angeles), 1999.
18. Sam Stanton and M.. Enkoji, "Justice Doesn't Make Death Easy to Watch," The Sacramento Bee, 5 May 1999:Al.
19. Diana Griego Erwin, "Killer's Family Are Victims Too," The Sacramento Bee, 4 May 1999:B1.
20. "Racial Bias Reported in Death Sentences," The Sacramento Bee, 18 May 1999:B8.
21. Michael J. Sniffen, "Racial, Geographic Flaws Found in Federal Death Penalty System," The Sacramento Bee, 13 Sept. 2000:A7.
22. "U.S. Pressured to End Death Penalty," National Catholic Reporter, 22 Oct. 1999:36.

23. Bryan Stevenson, "When Stones Go Flying," The Other Side, Vol. 30, No. 1, pp. 10–11.

24. Matthew B. Stannard, "Public Opinion Drives Death Penalty Policy," Tri-Valley Herald, 6 Dec. 1998: News–13.

25. Jon Matthews, "Death Penalty Support Dips; Execution Study Backed," The Sacramento Bee, 22 June 2000:A10.

26. Claire Cooper, "No 'Fast Track' for Most State Death Row Cases," The Sacramento Bee, 25 Jan. 2000:A3.

27. Claire Cooper, "In Executions, What May Witnesses See?," The Sacramento Bee, 15 Feb. 2000:A3.

28. Raymond Bonner and Ford Fessenden, "New Fuel in Death Penalty Debate," The Sacramento Bee, 22 Sept. 2000:A1.

29. Gerald D. Coleman, S.S., "The Death Penalty in California," The Redwood Crozier (Diocese of Santa Rosa), March 1999.

30. "The Gospel of Life and Capital Punishment" (1999), California Catholic Conferences of Bishops:1–3, 5.

31. "Statement of Conscience" (edited), California People of Faith Working Against the Death Penalty (for information: Office of Detention Ministry, Archdiocese of Los Angeles, 3424 Wilshire Blvd., L.A. 90010, (213) 637-7637).

32. Detention Ministry (Archdiocese Los Angeles).

Chapter IV

1. John 1:1–14; 12:44-50; 14:10–11.

2. Mark 1:14–15; John 3:16; John 4:14.

3. Howard Zehr, *Changing Lenses*, 1990 (Herald Press, Scottsdale, AZ), p. 135.

4. Howard Zehr, pp. 143–144.

5. Howard Zehr, p. 155.

6. Howard Zehr, pp. 141–142, 199–200.

7. Matthew 5:44-45.

8. Matthew 5:7.

9. Romans 5:8.

10. Matthew 22:34–40.

11. John 15:12-17.

12. Matthew 7:1–5.

13. Matthew 18:21–35.

14. Romans 13:8–10; Matthew 7:12.

15. 1 John 4:19–21.

16. Howard Zehr, pp. 46–50.

17. Luke 10:29–37.

18. Acts 9:1–5.

19. 1 Corinthians 12, 13.

20. Matthew 25:31–46.

21. Luke 19:1–10.

22. Matthew 9:9–13.

23. Matthew 23.

24. Luke 23: 33–43.

25. John 8:1–11.

26. Rev. Phillip Wogaman, "Eye of the Storm: A Pastor to the President Speaks Out," (John Knox Press, Louisville, KY), as quoted in the "National Catholic Reporter," 19 Jan. 1999:7.

27. Howard Zehr, pp. 152–153.

28. Matthew 12:1–14; Mark 3:1–12.

29. John 12:24.

30. Matthew 5:38–42.

31. Ephesians 4:26; Matthew 5:21–26.

32. Luke 7:18–23; Matthew 23.

33. Luke 15.

34. Sr. Helen Prejean, CSJ, author of "Dead Man Walking."

35. 1 Peter 1:17–21.

36. Matthew 25:14–30.

37. John 13:14–17.

38. Howard Zehr, pp. 136–137.

39. Psalm 130:3.

40. Romans 12:9–21.

41. Howard Zehr, pp. 151–152 (adapted).

Chapter V

1. "Changing Lenses" is the title of the definitive reference work on restorative justice by Howard Zehr, 1990, Scottsdale, PA:Herald Press.

2. New Zealand Catholic Bishops Conference, "Creating New Hearts:Moving from Retributive to Restorative Justice," Sept. 1, 1995, #'s 16, 8, 11.

3. Teresa Malcolm, "Activists Share Strategies for Ending the Death Penalty," National Catholic Reporter, 23 Apr 1999:3.

4. Malcom..

5. Michael J. Farrell, "They Say You Can Do Yourself a Favor Forgiving Others," National Catholic Reporter, 30 May 1997:9–11.

6. Changing Lenses, pp. 65–67.

7. Luke 11:33–36.

8. Luke 13:20–21.

9. Matthew 5:13.

10. Matthew 15:14.

11. Charles W. Colson, "Chicken Soup for the Christian Soul".

12. Jim Consedine, "A Justice Based on Healing," The Catholic Worker, 36 E. First St., NY, NY 10002, Jan–Feb 1996.
13. Changing Lenses, pp. 40–44.
14. Luke 19:1–10.
15. Changing Lenses, pp. 28-31.
16. *Catechism of the Catholic Church*, #2266.
17. Changing Lenses, p 34.
18. Robert McClory, "Reviving Energy for Action and Justice," National Catholic Reporter, 15, Jan. 1999:4.
19. "Restorative Justice," Center for Restorative Justice and Mediation, School of Social Work, Univ. of Minnesota, 386 McNeal Hall, 1985 Buford Ave., St. Paul, MN 55108, 1996:9.
20. Andrew Skotnicki, OCarm., "Their Real Roots Are Authentically Christian," The Tidings (Archdiocese of Los Angeles), 16 June 2000:3.
21. William M. DiMascio, "Seeking Justice: Crime and Punishment in America," Edna McConnell Clark Foundation, 1996.

Chapter VI

1. Ella Cara Deloria, "Waterlily," (Lincoln, Nebr.: Univ. of Nebraska Press, 1988), pp. 191–194, as related by Elaine M. Prevallet, S.L., "A Kinship Appeal," Weavings, Vol. XIII, No. 6, 1998, pp. 40–42.
2. Claire Cooper, "Mediation Program Helps Offenders, Victims Find Peace," The Sacramento Bee, 1 Jan. 1999:A1.
3. Tom Kenworthy, "Gay Victim's Parents Broker Life Sentence for Killer," Washington Post, as reported in The Sacramento Bee, 5 Nov. 1999:A6.
4. The Orange County Register, Editorial, 29 Mar. 1999: Metro 6.
5. Detention Ministry (Archdiocese of Los Angeles), Jan–Feb. 2000:5.
6. Howard Zehr, *Changing Lenses* (Herald Press, Scottsdale, AZ, 1990), p. 216.
7. Howard Zehr, p. 186.
8. Howard Zehr, p. 199.
9. Howard Zehr, pp. 218–220.
10. Howard Zehr, p. 227.
11. "Restorative Justice," America, 26 Feb. 2000:7–11.
12. Claire Cooper, "Mediation Program Helps…," A22.
13. Gil Jose Duran, "Communities Make Youths Accountable For Offense," The Sacramento Bee, 23 Aug. 1998:A5.
14. Sherri Day, "At-Risk Kids Get Police 'Treatment' to Ward Off Violence," The Sacramento Bee, 18 July 1999:B1.
15. Claire Cooper.
16. "Teens will Sit in Judgment of Teens," The Sacramento Bee, 3 Dec. 1997.
17. Claire Cooper.

18. "Restorative Justice" (1966), Center for Restorative Justice & Mediation, School of Social Work, Univ. of Minnesota, 386 McNeal Hall, 1985 Buford Ave., St. Paul, MN 55108–6144, (612) 624–4923.

19. "Restorative Justice."

20. Howard Zehr, pp. 161–167.

21. Yvonne Chiu, "Yolo Judge's Novel Idea Redefines Family Court," The Sacramento Bee, 23 Jan. 1999:A1.

22. "Beyond Bars: Correctional Reforms to Lower Prison Costs and Reduce Crime," The Little Hoover Commission Report on Corrections in California (600 J St., Ste. 260, Sacramento, CA 95814), Jan. 1998, p. 41.

23. Eric Lichtblau, "Re-Entry Courts to Reduce Crime by Parolees," Los Angeles Times as reported by The Sacramento Bee, 11 Aug. 1999:A10.

24. Ada Pecos Melton, "Indigenous Ways Are Restorative Justice Models," Newsletter of the Minnesota Dept. of Corrections Restorative Justice Program, April 1996. (1450 Energy Park Dr., Ste. 200, St. Paul, MN 55108–5219).

25. "Beyond Bars," p. 39–41.

26. Ramon Coronado, "House Arrest Sentences on Rise in County," The Sacramento Bee, 5 Jan. 2000:B1.

27. "Mothers and Their Kids Behind Bars," The Communicator (California Men's Colony, San Luis Obispo), Feb–Mar. 2000.

28. "Planned Court Gets Funds," The Sacramento Bee, 23 June 1999:B2.

29. Herbert J. Hoelter and Barry R. Holman, "Listen to the Poor Locked Behind Bars," The Sacramento Bee, 14 Aug. 1999:B7. (Hoelter directs the National Center on Institutions and Alternatives (703) 684–0373.)

30. Muriel Dobbin, "Drug Sentencing Rules Draw Judicial Fire," The Sacramento Bee, 6 June 1999:A4.

31. "Beyond Bars," p. 43.

32. "Probation Program, Not Prison, for Addicts," New York Times, 21 Apr. 1999.

33. Katherine E. Finkelstein, "N.Y. Launches Program to Keep Addicts Out of Jail," New York Times as reported in The Sacramento Bee, 23 June 00:A16.

34. "Treatment, Not Jail," The Sacramento Bee, Editorial, 17 Mar. 1999:B6.

35. Robert D. Davila and Kevin Yamamura, "County Approves Program for Mentally Ill Offenders," The Sacramento Bee, 21 July 1999:B1.

36. "Mental Health Bill Signed By Davis," The Sacramento Bee, 20 Sept. 2000:A6.

37. "Beyond Bars," p. 40.

38. "Beyond Bars," pp. 30-31.

39. Neal Peirce, "A Republican Takes On Prison-Industrial Complex," The Sacramento Bee,13 Feb. 2000:I3.

40. David S. Broder, "To Fight Crime, Play to People's Possibilities," The Sacramento Bee, 24 Mar. 1999:B9.

41. Andy Furillo, "Prison Drug Treatment Unpopular, But It Works," The Sacramento Bee, 4 Feb. 1999:A1.

42. Peter Schrag, "Drug Law Reform Is the Message Within Proposition 36," The Sacramento Bee, 13 Sept. 2000:B7.

43. "State Searches for Ways to Implement Drug Treatment," Ventura County Star, 13 Nov. 2000, A4.

44. "Misguided Drug Policy," The Sacramento Bee, Editorial, 30 Dec. 1998.

45. Susan Milligan, "Gore Proposes Treatment for Drug—Addiction," The Sacramento Bee, 3 May 2000:A6.

46. Dennis Love, "Faith A Rising Factor in Presidential Bids," The Sacramento Bee, 6 June 1999:A1.

47. "Beyond Bars," pp.46–49.

48. "Prison Education," The Sacramento Bee, 12 Aug. 2000:B6.

49. Ramon Coronado, "Lawyers' New Case: Helping Parolees Thrive," The Sacramento Bee, 25 Dec. 2000, B1.

50. John J. DiIulio, Jr. "Drug War Follies: 2 Million Prisoners Are Enough," Wall Street Journal as reported by The Sacramento Bee, 4 Apr. 1999: L11.

51. Copies may be ordered from the Publications Office, United States Catholic Conference, 3211 Fourth St., NE, Washington, D.C. 20017.

Chapter VII

1. Sr. Suzanne Steffen, CSJ, Women's Advocate, "Detention Ministry, Archdiocese of Los Angeles.

2. Patrick J. Morris, Superior Court Judge, San Bernardino County, CA. "Justice Jottings" (newsletter of the Presbyterian Church U.S.A.) Criminal Justice program, Summer: 1996.

3. 1 Peter 2:4–5.

4. "Constitution on the Church in the Modern World," #43.

5. "Sharing Catholic Social Teaching: Challenges and Directions—Reflections of the U.S. Catholic Bishops," as quoted in "Ten Building Blocks of Catholic Social Teaching," William J. Byron, SJ, Amercia:31 October 1998, p. 9.

6. Cardinal Joseph Bernardin's image of respect life issues as being of "Whole Cloth", as was Jesus' garment which was not torn apart when the soldiers divided his belongings among themselves.

7. Byron, p. 9 (see endnote #5 above).

8. Byron, p. 10–11. *Reflections*: "Sharing Catholic Social Teachings: Challenges and Directions–Reflections of the U.S. Catholic Bishops."

9. Principles #9 and #10 are taken from the companion document to "Reflections": "Summary Report of the Task force on Catholic Social Teaching and Education."

10. Repetitive refrain at the end of each admonition and challenge to the churches in Revelation 2 and 3.

11. "Imagine All Bishops Going to Prison," Editorial, National Catholic Reporter, 7 May 1999:28.

12. Nancy Westlund, "Catholic Leaders Make Rare Visit to San Quentin Death Row," The Tydings (Archdiocese of Los Angeles), 26 March 1999:5.

13. Lesie Wirpsa, "Trying to Make Justice Work for Women," National Catholic Reporter, 29 May 1998:12–13.

14. Lou Torok, "Keeping the Faith in Prison," America, 27 Feb. 1999:16.

15. Bryan Apper, "Fresno Catholic Worker Provides Detention and Outreach Ministries," Restoring Justice (Archdiocese of Los Angeles), Spring 1998. (St. Benedict Catholic Worker, 4022 N. Cheryl Ave., Fresno, CA 93705–2201, (209) 229–6410, SBCS@juno.com).

16. "Campaign Calls for Bell Tolls at Executions," National Catholic Reporter, 3 Nov. 2000:13.

17. Jennifer Finn, "Saint Mary's College Professors Volunteer in Unique Prison Education Program," St. Mary's Alumni Newsletter early 2000.

18. Lupita Figueiredo, "Offering Friendship and Peace to the Incarcerated," Catholic San Francisco, 26 May 2000:7.

19. Detention Ministry (Archdiocese of Los Angeles), March-April 1999. For information on the academy, Bro. Modesto or Teresa Duran, (323) 261–9712.

20. Diana Griego Erwin, "A Wake Up Call to Female Inmates," The Sacramento Bee, 14 March 1999:B1. (Sister's Keep Liaison, (916) 553–5041).

21. "The Inside Out Network," The Redwood Crozier (Diocese of Santa Rosa), Feb. 2000:14.

22. "Soledad Parish Remembers the Incarcerated," Detention Ministry, Jan–Feb. 2000:5.

23. For more information, e-mail http://www.sistersonline.org/multi.cgi?multi=us_issues.

24. For information, contact the Archdiocese of Los Angeles, Office of Detention Ministry, 3424 Wilshire Blvd., Los Angeles, CA 90010.

25. Leslie Mladinich, "Prison Ministry Brings Joy to Dublin Inmates," Tri-Valley Herald, 26 Dec. 1998:4-Local.

26. For information: Mike Kelley, Contemplative Fellowship, P.O. Box 441, Folsom, CA 95763–0441.

27. Copies may be ordered from the Publications Office, United States Catholic Conference, 3211 Fourth St., NE, Washington, D.C. 20017.

28. Restoring Justice, (Archdiocese of Los Angeles) Sept–Oct 1997:1.

Chapter VIII

1. Luke 15:11-32.
2. Based on "The Frog King" by Jacob and Wilhelm Grimm.
3. John L. Allen, Jr., "In Jail's Rotunda, John Paul Calls for Liberation," National Catholic Reporter, 28 July 2000:5.

Appendix—A

PRE-QUIZ—ANSWERS

14. d) 2 million.

15. d) People are serving 25 years-to-life for crimes committed 20 years apart, while a teenager, for stealing pizza, for possession of small amounts of drugs for personal use. "Three strikes" is not limited to serious or violent crimes.

16. b) 71% improve public schools, 62% increase job opportunities, 54% increase sentences.

17. b) Women, two-thirds of whom have children under 18 of which only 25% are being cared for by their father.

18. a) Yes. The U.S. prison population is composed of 44% African Americans (12% of general population), 36% white (74%), 18% Hispanic (10%).

19. c) 50–75% of inmates cannot read; 33% have not completed high school.

20. d) California's 1997 recidivism rate was 74.5%, the highest in the nation.

21. a) Indigent inmates facing life in prison received a maximum $144.50 worth of legal representation while being consider for parole.

22. a) Yes. African American's who kill whites receive the death penalty at a rate 11 times higher than whites who kill blacks. Of 500 prisoners executed between 1977–1998, 81.8% had killed a white person, while the number of white and black homicide victims was almost the same.

23. d) For all these, and other, reasons, alternatives to incarceration are increasingly being used. This is the good news in an otherwise mostly bad news system.

Appendix—B

CATHOLIC SOCIAL TEACHING
FOURTEEN MAJOR LESSONS
(See Chapter VII)

1. **Link of religious and social dimensions of life.** The "social"——the human construction of the world—is not "secular" in the sense of being outside of God's plan, but is intimately involved with the dynamic Reign of God.

2. **Dignity of the human person.** Made in the image of God, persons have a preeminent place in the social order. Human dignity can be recognized and protected only in community with others.

3. **Political and economic rights.** All persons enjoy inalienable rights, which are political-legal and social-economic.

4. **Option for the poor.** A preferential love should be shown to the poor, whose needs and rights are given special attention in God's eyes.

5. **Link of love and justice.** Love of neighbor is an absolute demand for justice, because charity must manifest itself in actions and structures which respect human dignity, protect human rights and facilitate human development. To promote justice is to transform structures which block love.

6. **Promotion of the common good.** The common good is the sum total of all those conditions of social living which make it possible for persons to achieve the perfection of their humanity. Individual rights are always experienced within the context of the promotion of the common good.

7. **Subsidiarity.** Responsibilities and decisions should be attended to as close as possible at the level of individual initiative in local communities and institutions.

8. **Political participation.** Democratic participation in decision making is the best way to respect the dignity and liberty of people. The government is the instrument by which people cooperate together in order to achieve the common good.

9. **Economic justice.** The economy is for the people and the resources of the earth are to be shared equally by all. Labor takes precedence over both capital and technology in the production process. Just wages and the right of workers to organize are to be respected.

10. **Stewardship.** All property has a "social mortgage." By our work we are co-creators in the continuing development of the earth.

11. **Solidarity.** We belong to one human family. As such we have mutual obligations to promote the rights and development of all people across communities, nations and the world.

12. **Promotion of Peace.** Peace is the fruit of justice and is dependent upon right order among persons and among nations.

13. **Work.** Work can and must serve an individual's humanity and dignity. Work is the way that persons share in the activity of God.

14. **Liberation.** Liberation from oppressive social, political and economic situations and structures is an important part of the church's activity.

Catholic Social Teaching, Our Best Kept Secret (Part1, #4)
DeBerri, Henriot & Schulteis

Appendix—C

Measuring Restorative Justice

The continuum on the following page will evaluate personal, family, political and judicial processes to determine if they are implementing restorative justice.

The arrows indicate these are not simple either/or situations, nor ones which can't be improved.

Score_____:

26 or Less—Justice response dominated by government and very costly: emotionally, spiritually, and financially. High fear in the community. Many mini-communities alienated and angry. Very high crime rate.

52 or More—Justice response balanced between government and community. Mini and macro communities empowered to participate in and contribute to the emotional, spiritual, and financial health of *all* the members of the community. Very low crime rate.

Taken from VORP News, July 1996.

Victim Offender Reconciliation Program,

(209) 291-1120. VORP grants permission to reproduce these pages.

Moral wrong of crime (violation of persons and relationships) ignored or minimized	1 Not RJ RJ – 1 – 2 – 3 – 4 – 5 –	Moral wrong of crime (violation of persons and relationships) recognized
Victim, community, and offender safety concerns ignored	2 Not RJ RJ – 1 – 2 – 3 – 4 – 5 –	Victim, community, and offender concerns primary
Disempower victims, offenders, and their communities to act constructively	3 Not RJ RJ – 1 – 2 – 3 – 4 – 5 –	Empower victims, offenders, and their communities to act constructively
Making things as right as possible? secondary concern	4 Not RJ RJ – 1– 2 – 3 – 4 – 5 –	Primary focus on ?making things as right as possible? (repair injuries, relationships, and physical damage)
Primary focus on violation of law	5 Not RJ RJ – 1 – 2 – 3 – 4 – 5 –	Violation of law secondary, backup
Victim wounds and healing ignored	6 Not RJ RJ – 1 – 2 – 3 – 4 – 5 –	Victim wounds and healing important
Offender wounds and healing ignored	7 Not RJ RJ – 1 – 2 – 3 – 4 – 5 –	Offender wounds and healing important
Primary decisions and activity between offender and government; offender family, victim, and community left out	8 Not RJ RJ – 1 – 2 – 3 – 4 – 5 –	Primary decisions and activity between offender and victim (or substitutes and their communities, with government help as needed)
Actions of officials with coercive power or in positions of authority left unchecked	9 Not RJ RJ – 1 – 2 – 3 – 4 – 5 –	All actions tested by whether they are reasonable, related, and respectful
Government coercive and/or authority structures utilized as primary response; victims, offenders, and community left out of process	10 Not RJ RJ – 1 – 2 – 3 – 4 – 5 –	Government coercive and/or authority structures utilized as backup when victim or offender not cooperative or if community process is viewed as unfair by victim or offender
Coercion assumed as primary mode of relating to offenders; orders are given; invitations to offender to be cooperative are not offered; no attempt at agreements	11 Not RJ RJ – 1 – 2 – 3 – 4 – 5 –	Invitations to offender to be cooperative are primary; agreements preferred; coercion used as a backup when offender is not cooperative
Placements focus on restrictions and following orders	12 Not RJ RJ – 1 – 2 – 3 – 4 – 5–	Placements when needed for safety and/or training and equipping for living in community
Religious/faith community not involved in justice process	13 Not RJ RJ – 1 – 2 – 3 – 4 – 5 –	Religious/faith community encouraged and invited into cooperative aspects of justice process

Score_____

Appendix—D

A Restorative Justice Yardstick

1. Do victims experience justice?

- Do victims have sufficient opportunities to tell their truth to relevant listeners?
- Do victims receive needed compensation or restitution?
- Is the injustice adequately acknowledged?
- Are victims sufficiently protected against further violation?
- Does the outcome adequately reflect the severity of the offense?
- Do victims receive adequate information about the crime, the offender, and the legal process?
- Do victims have a voice in the legal process?
- Is the experience of justice adequately public?
- Do victims receive adequate support from others?
- Do victims' families receive adequate assistance and support?
- Are other needs—material, psychological, and spiritual—being addressed?

2. Do offenders experience justice?

- Are offenders encouraged to understand and take responsibility for what they have done?
- Are misattributions challenged?
- Are offenders given encouragement and opportunities to make things right?
- Are offenders given opportunities to participate in the process?
- Are offenders encouraged to change their behavior?
- Is there a mechanism for monitoring or verifying changes?

- Are offenders' needs being addressed?
- Do offenders' families receive support and assistance?

3. Is the victim-offender relationship addressed?

- Is there an opportunity for victims and offenders to meet, if appropriate?
- Is there an opportunity for victims and offenders to exchange information about the event and about one another?

4. Are community concerns being taken into account?

- Is the process and the outcome sufficiently public?
- Is community protection being addressed?
- Is there a need for restitution or a symbolic action for the community?
- Is the community represented in some way in the legal process?
- Is the future addressed?
- Is there provision for solving the problems that led to this event?
- Is there provision for solving problems caused by this event?
- Have future intentions been addressed?
- Are there provisions for monitoring and verifying outcomes and for problem solving?

Source: Howard Zehr, *Changing Lenses* (Scottsdale, Pennsylvania: Herald Press, 1990)

Appendix—E

CROSS-REFERENCE to *Responsibility, Rehabilitation, and Restoration: A Catholic Perspective on Crime and Criminal Justice*
A Statement of the Catholic Bishops of the United States, November 15, 2000.

Topics and issues addressed in **RRR** are found in many sections of **PJSE**, and are repetitive and interwoven throughout both resources. Listed below are the primary **PJSE** chapter references and sample section references to the **RRR** Table of Contents.

1 The full text may be ordered from the USCC Publications Office, 3211 Fourth St. NE, Washington, D.C., Publication No. 5-394, ISBN 1-57455-394-1, or call 800-235-8722

Restorative Justice Resources

Major Books

Changing Lenses (1990), Howard Zehr. (The basic resource and research on restorative justice.) Herald Press, Scottsdale, PA., SBN 0–8361–3512–1.

Restorative Justice, Healing the Effects of Crime (1995), Jim Consedine, Ploughshares Publications. ISBN 0–473–02992–8.

Victim Meets Offender (1994), Mark Umbreit. (First large multi-site including California—evaluation of victim-offender mediation programs working with juvenile courts.) Criminal Justice Press, P.O. Box 249, Monsey, NY 10952. ISBN 1–881–79802–X.

Studies and Reports

Balanced and Restorative Justice Program Summary (1994), Gordon Bazemore & Mark Umbreit, Office of Juvenile Justice and Delinquency Prevention, Dept. of Justice, Washington, D.C.

Restorative Community Justice: A Call to Action (1995), National Organization for Victim Assistance, Washington, D.C.

Restoring Justice (50 min. video—$5 plus postage), Presbyterian Church for the National Council of Churches, 1–800–524-2612, Product #7263096720.

Behind Bars: Correction Reforms to Lower Costs and Reduce Crime (1998), Little Hoover Commission ($5 includes shipping) 660 J St., Suite 260, Sacramento, CA 95814.

Report on Prison and Parole Reform (Feb. 1998), Legislative Analyst, 925 L St., Suite 1000, Sacramento, CA 95814, (916) 322–2072.

Magazines

The Other Side, $29.50 yr., (bimonthly Christian faith-based social justice magazine.), 300 W. Apsley St., Philadelphia, PA 19914, (215) 849–2178.

POZ, $24.95 yr. (Prison concerns), P.O. Box 417, Mt. Morris, IL 61054–8406.

Sojourners, $30 yr. (Christian application of social justice to life and action.), 2401 15th St., NW, Washington, D.C. 20009.

The National Prison Project Journal ($2 prisoners, $30 others, quarterly articles, reports, legal & legislative news.), 1875 Connecticut Ave., N.W., Ste. 410, Washington, D.C. 20009.

Friends Committee on Legislation of California Newsletter, 926 J St., Rm. 707, Sacramento, CA 95814–2707.

Religious Organizations

Mennonite Central Committee, Office of Community Justice, P.O. Box 500, Akron, PA 17501, (717) 859–3889.

Presbyterian Criminal Justice Program, 100 Witherspoon St., Louisville, KY 40202–1396, (502) 569–5810.

United States Catholic Conference, Office of Social Development & World Peace, 3211 Fourth St., NE, Washington, D.C. 20017.

Catholic Center for Restorative Justice, Archdiocese of Los Angeles, 3424 Wilshire Blvd., Los Angeles, CA 90010–2241, (213) 637–7637.

American Friends Service Committee, (Advocacy, education, organizing for criminal justice.), 1501 Cherry St., Philadelphia, PA, 19102–1479.

Public and Private Organizations

Center for Restorative Justice & Mediation and The Balanced and Restorative Justice Project (resource packet sent on request), School of Social Work, 386 McNeal Hall, University of Minnesota, 1985 Buford Avenue, St. Paul, MN 55108-6144, (612) 625–4288; e-mail: ctr4rjm@che2.che.umn.edu.

Minnesota Department of Corrections, Office of Restorative Justice (resource packet sent on request), 1450 Energy Park Dr., Ste. 200, St. Paul, MN55108–5219, (612) 624–0338.

National Organization for Victim Assistance, 1757 Park Road, N.W., Washington, C.D. 20010, (202) 232–6682, e-mail: NOVA@access.digex.net.

Victim Offender Mediation Association, 777 So. Main St., Ste. 200, Orange, CA 92668, (714)–836-8100, e-mail: vorpoc@igc.apc.org

Murder Victims Families for Reconciliation,2161 Massachusetts Avenue, Cambridge, MA 02140, (603) 926–2737.

Pro-Family Advocates (inmate family concerns), P.O. Box 17892, Long Beach, CA 90807–7892, e-mail: ProfamilyAdvocates@juno.com.

Center for Peacemaking and Conflict Studies, Fresno Pacific University, 1717 So. Chestnut Avenue, Fresno, CA 93702, (209) 455–5840.

California Prison Focus (Provides educational resources and speakers on prison concerns), 2489 Mission St., Ste. 28, San Francisco, CA 94110, (415) 452–3359, 821–6545.

Prisoner's Rights Union (annual membership: $10 prisoners, $35 others), (Education and advocacy; monitors legislation, class action suites, Dept of Corrections), P.O. Box 1019, Sacramento, CA 95812–1019, (916) 441–4214.

Californians to Amend 3 Strikes (CATS) (Advocacy to amend 3-Strikes; advocacy for prisoners and families.), 2729 N. Bristol St. B5–112, Santa Ana, CA 92706, (714) 541–2073, e-mail: mucsuss@sos101.com.

The Sentencing Project (Works to develop sentencing programs promoting alternatives to incarceration.), 918 F St., N.W., Ste. 501, Washington, D.C. 20004, (202) 628–0871, Web site: http://www.sentencingproject.org /*e-mail: washdc@sentencingproject.org*

Public and Private Organizations

Victim Offender Reconciliation Program (VORP) (Trains and provides mediators.), 2529 Willow Ave., Clovis, CA 93612, (209) 291–1120, Web site: http://www.fresno.edu/pacs/rjm.html.

Alternatives to Violence Project (A.P.) (Provides training, workshops, support community and resources for inmates while in prison and after release. Ex-offenders and others helping parolees successfully transition back into society.), National Office: A.P.–USA, 821 Euclid Ave., Syracuse, NY 13210, (713) 747–9999, e-mail: avp@avpusa.org. Publications: A.P. Distribution Service, 844 John Fowler Rd.,Plainfield, VT 05667, (802) 45–-4675, e-mail: ataplow@bigfoot.com.

Families to Amend California's Three Strikes (FACTS), (323) 298–0510, e-mail: http://www.facts.com.

Government Agencies & Officials

Office of the Governor, State Capitol, Sacramento, CA 95814, (916) 445–2841, e-mail: graydavis@governor.ca.gov.

State Senate/Assembly, (check front of phone book under "State" for your legislators.), State Capitol, Sacramento, CA 95814.

Board of Prison Terms, 428 J St., 6th Floor, Sacramento, CA 95814.

California Dept. of Corrections, Cal Terhune, Director, P.O. Box 942883, Sacramento, CA 94283-0001, (916) 445-7682.

Printed in the United States
131883LV00001B/124/A

9 780595 176540